For Charles —
with warmest regards —
and best wishes

Jim Laney

For Charles —
With gratitude for your
moral leadership at Emory.

F. Stuart Gulley

May 2002

THE ACADEMIC PRESIDENT
AS MORAL LEADER

James T. Laney at Emory University, 1977–1993

F. Stuart Gulley

MERCER UNIVERSITY PRESS
MMI

ISBN 0-86554-725-4
MUP/H544

© 2001 Mercer University Press
6316 Peake Road
Macon, Georgia 31210-3960
All rights reserved

First Edition.

∞The paper used in this publication meets the
minimum requirements of American National Standard
for Information Sciences—Permanence of Paper for Printed
Library Materials, ANSI Z39.48-1992.

Library of Congress Cataloging-in-Publication Data

Gulley, F. Stuart.
The academic president as moral leader: James T. Laney at Emory
University, 1977-1993 / by F. Stuart Gulley.
p. cm.
Includes bibliographical references and index.
ISBN 0-86554-725-4
1. Laney, James T. 2. Emory University—President—Biography. I.
Title.

LD1751.E3817 L36 2001
378.758'231—dc21

2001030682

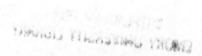

TABLE OF CONTENTS

ACKNOWLEDGMENTS

This book is a revision of the dissertation I wrote for the completion of the Ph.D. in Higher Education at Georgia State University. To the members of my faculty committee—Dr. Philo Hutcheson (my advisor), Dr. Thomas Frank (of Emory University), Dr. Al McWilliams, and Dr. Wayne Urban—who read and commented on the manuscript, and whose criticisms I have faithfully attempted to incorporate here, I am deeply grateful. I also am indebted to Dr. Linda Buchanan, Dr. Sam Hornsby, Dr. Judson Ward, Dr. James Gustafson, and Dr. Steven Gunter, who offered their own questions, comments, and corrections, after reading the manuscript. Their feedback has improved the final product immeasurably, although I accept full responsibility for the inadequacies that remain.

The acknowledgment section of my dissertation ran six pages in length, expressing my deep gratitude to members of my family, colleagues at Emory University, LaGrange College, and the Troup County Archives, persons I interviewed about Laney, and Laney himself. Space here does not permit me to acknowledge them again personally, but they know who they are and I want to express again my profound thanks for what they did to assist me over the years this book was developing. A special thank you must go to Ginger Cain, university archivist at the Robert W. Woodruff Library of Emory, and Ann Borden, director of photography at Emory, for their assistance with the photographs included here. Dr. Arthur Robinson of the Banks Library of LaGrange College did yeoman's work in compiling the index and reviewing the manuscript for which I am forever in his debt. Also, I wish to thank my executive secretary, Lydia Wheitsel, for all that she has done for me personally and professionally, and for her "extra-mile" efforts with this manuscript.

Finally, I want to thank the editors of Mercer University Press for their editorial enhancements to the text. Especially I wish to thank them for their conviction that the accomplishments of Laney as a moral leader at Emory are great enough to our state and our country, to higher education, and to the church, that his story deserves to be published.

F. Stuart Gulley
LaGrange College
LaGrange, GA
August 2000

For the trustees, faculty, staff, and students of LaGrange College,
all of whom are moral leaders engaged in an exciting quest to make
LaGrange College Georgia's premier private liberal arts and sciences college.

INTRODUCTION

Reading the numerous biographies of university and college presidents since the founding of Harvard is one of the methods researchers employ to understand the history of higher education in the United States. The quality of many of these works does not compare to today's rigorous academic standards because they were written mostly for purposes of institutional memory and/or to glorify the actions of the president while in office. Still, quality works exist, such as Mary Ann Dzuback's biography of Robert M. Hutchins at Chicago (1929–1951), Richard Storr's biography of William Rainey Harper at Chicago (1892–1906), Hugh Hawkins' biography of Charles W. Eliot at Harvard (1869–1909), and Wayne Urban's biography of Horace Mann Bond at Fort Valley (1939–1945) and Lincoln (1945–1957).[1] Each of these works gives significant insight into the personal, cultural, social, economic, political, and institutional dynamics at work in the administrations of these individuals. Even the major historical works about higher education, such as those by Laurence Veysey and Frederick Rudolph, give significant attention to the achievements of college presidents as a way of understanding the progress of higher education in this country.[2]

Sadly, there is a dearth of scholarly work about college presidents who have served in the latter part of the twentieth century. This lacking can be attributed to the relative newness of these administrations that have yet to capture the attention of scholars of higher education. It can also be attributed to the fact that the tenure of college presidents in recent decades has declined dramatically, making for few truly outstanding university presidencies in this period. A recent study by the American Council on Education showed that the average tenure of presidents in doctoral universities in 1986 was 6.1 years and fell to five years in 1995.[3] Thus, the forty year tenure of Eliot, or fourteen year tenure of Harper (who died while in office), or twenty-two year tenure of Hutchins, or twelve year tenure of Bond (at Lincoln) are anomalies today, especially at major research universities. A review of Dr. James T. Laney's leadership as president of Emory University from 1977 until 1993, such as I propose to do here, will, I hope, add to the literature of scholarly biographies of latter twentieth-century academic presidents, and enhance our understanding of some of the dynamics of higher education in this era.

A number of reasons compel me to choose Laney as my topic, not the least of which was my intimate knowledge of his presidency at Emory while I was both a student and an administrator there. The overriding reason for Laney as my focus, however, is twofold. First, Laney more than any research university president of his era believed that an academic president was fundamentally a moral leader. The moral authority of the president, for Laney, derived from the fact that a liberal arts education in and of itself was a moral endeavor. Thus, for Laney, the president was to demonstrate those qualities of moral leadership that would have a leavening effect throughout the institution. Laney's commitment to the moral dimensions of the academic presidency was stated repeatedly in speeches and articles and demonstrated in most of his actions while president.

A second reason for focusing on the Laney presidency is that during his administration Emory underwent a remarkable transformation from a solid regional teaching institution to a major national research university. I will explore the various reasons for this change, but among them now can be noted Laney's sixteen year tenure, an indication of his popularity among the university's various constituent groups in an era when, as noted earlier, presidents lasted on average six years or less. A second factor in Laney's transformation of Emory was his success in fundraising, especially the securing of the Woodruff gift of $105 million in 1979, at the time the largest gift ever in US philanthropy. As evidence of Emory's transformation under Laney, both prior to and soon after his departure in 1993, Emory was ranked among the top twenty national research universities in the country by *US News and World Report*; its Carnegie classification was changed to Research I from Research II, and it was admitted to the elite Association of American Universities (AAU).

Absent the external opinions of Emory's quality as an institution, the internal numbers tell a story of impressive growth and change as well. During Laney's tenure, Emory was transformed by most salient measures. The endowment grew by 1000 percent, from $178 million to $1.76 billion;[4] college student enrollment increased to 7,700 from 3,760;[5] faculty appointments increased 67 percent;[6] and new buildings were erected at a breathtaking rate, adding 2.6 million square feet.[7] Even more impressive, these changes occurred during an era when economic uncertainties, changing accreditation standards, increased government scrutiny, and political correctness challenged even the strongest of institutions. While some universities faced the difficult task of retrenchment in the face of these challenges, during Laney's administration Emory managed to move forward.

In many ways, Emory's growth and change was not unlike that of some of the most noted American universities of the late nineteenth and the early twentieth centuries, such as Chicago and Harvard. In fact, during Laney's tenure, outside observers, especially in reference to the use of the Woodruff gift, referred to Emory as a "new Chicago."[8] Even Laney occasionally made similar comparisons by referencing statements of William Rainey Harper, the first president of the University of Chicago, 1892–1906. In an interview, Laney had this to say about the comparison with Harper: "I have no right to make the connection with William

Rainey Harper. He was a minister, and he established a really, an absolutely first-rate university. I used to make that connection. I said, 'Atlanta's sort of like Chicago at the turn of the century, and we've got Woodruff money like Rockefeller, and we've got a preacher as the president. And we're going to do this.'"[9]

In telling the story of Laney's leadership at Emory, I will draw occasionally on the comparison of Emory to Chicago because I believe it to be apt, given the growth that took place at both institutions and the support of generous donors, such as Rockefeller at Chicago and Woodruff at Emory. The combination of generous donors, visionary and aggressive presidents, such as Harper and then later Hutchins at Chicago and Laney at Emory, and urban settings coming into their own, such as Chicago early in the twentieth century and Atlanta in the 1980s, makes a strong case for this comparison.[10] Of course there is much that is different in these comparisons. Chicago was starting from scratch under Harper's administration. Laney was Emory's sixth University president since 1915. Thus, Laney had much more infrastructure on which to build. During the tenure of Hutchins the faculty had much more say in the governance of the institution, as is seen by the presence of voting faculty on the search committee when Hutchins was named president,[11] and the absence of any faculty on the presidential search that selected Laney. Laney's impact on Emory was greater than Hutchins' on Chicago, as at Chicago the budget was a source of constant concern, and relations with faculty were continually contentious.[12] Also, the eras of early 1900s and the 1980s were entirely different culturally, politically, and economically. The demands that presidents faced in these varying milieus at times called for varying leadership styles. Harper and Hutchins, for instance, did not have to face the more stringent accrediting standards, the demands and opportunities of inclusivity, and the threats of litigation that challenged Laney. Yet, each of these presidents commanded central stage in the operation of their institutions. While I will rely on comparisons to Harper, Hutchins, and others to tell Laney's story, it should also be noted that I believe that Laney and other presidents of his era should be understood and appreciated independent of presidents of other generations because of the differences inherent in each era. Yet, the comparisons are helpful to understand how Laney's leadership occurred in the context of the thousands of academic presidents prior to his tenure.

While drawing occasionally on secondary source material for telling the story of Laney's leadership at Emory, I will principally tell the story based on archival materials found at Emory's Robert W. Woodruff Library and oral interviews with those who worked closely with Laney. In all, Laney left behind seventy-five boxes of files and official records of his actions while president. I will draw on insights gleaned from these files, especially the manuscripts from his speeches to civic groups, professional organizations, commencements and baccalaureates, faculty meetings, and parent groups. In addition, I conducted approximately fifteen oral interviews with members of Laney's senior staff, former faculty and former trustees, and three interviews with Laney himself.

My analysis of the various sources of information results in the following six chapters to tell as fully as possible the story of Laney's leadership while at Emory. It should be noted that these chapters represent a biography of Laney's leadership at Emory. I do not intend to present an institutional history of Emory. While I believe that what I write here will have value for understanding the institutional progress Emory made during this sixteen year period, it does not provide the comprehensive detail of developments at Emory that one would expect from an institutional history.

Chapter 1 tells about Laney's rise to the presidency of Emory in 1977. It does so by giving information on Laney's life, including his family, educational experiences, and employment history. It will examine Laney's background as a Southern-born boy, receiving all of his higher education training at Yale University,[13] then becoming a missionary to Korea and afterward rising through the higher education ranks—first at Vanderbilt and then Emory[14]—to become president. This chapter will also provide insight into the historical and political dynamics at work at Emory during the presidential search that resulted in Laney's selection.

Chapter 2 gives considerable detail about Laney's vision for Emory, namely his concern for the importance and strengthening of a liberal arts education as a moral endeavor. This vision was expressed in numerous settings through speeches and articles. A review of these speeches and articles will show how Laney articulated a vision of a church-related liberal arts education that moved beyond giving students credentials for a career. Laney's vision directed Emory to develop in students character and morals intended to make them effective and contributing citizens of society. In addition to what Laney articulated, I will examine those influences on his life that were instrumental in his conception of the purposes of higher learning, and conclude with an analysis of his efforts in these presentations.

No review of Laney's leadership at Emory is complete without attention to the $105 million Woodruff gift he helped secure in 1979, which is the topic of chapter 3. I will examine the nature of Emory's and Laney's relationship to the Woodruff brothers, what finally inspired the gift, and how the gift was put to use. The decision to delay for two years the spending of any of the gift so that the University could engage in a comprehensive institutional review to determine its strengths and weaknesses proved to be significant also, and will occupy some of my attention.

Chapter 4 tells the story of the transformation of Emory between 1977 and 1993. It does so by relating briefly some of the history of Emory prior to Laney's appointment. Then my analysis shows how Laney's administration falls into three phases as he attempted to make Emory into a major research university. Phase one from 1977 until 1980 was the period of assessing need, expressing the vision, and securing funding for the implementation of Laney's vision. Phase two from 1981 until 1986 was the era of the college and the student, when Laney attempted to strengthen the college and its liberal arts program, which he believed to be the core of the university. Phase three from 1987 until 1993 was the period of the graduate school and the faculty, where Emory's star began to rise prominently, especially as the Woodruff funds were put to judicious use to attract bright students and renowned faculty. This chapter will conclude with an analysis of Laney's efforts using budgetary information and student data gathered by the office of institutional research.

To appreciate the growth of Emory and Laney's efforts at providing moral leadership, it is appropriate to focus some discussion on the challenges he faced while in office and how he addressed them. In chapter 5, then, particular attention will be paid to the university's relationship to the church,[15] including Glenn Memorial United Methodist Church, as well as concerns expressed about alcohol on campus, pornography sold in the campus bookstore, and the inclusion of sexual orientation in the university's equal opportunity statement. A second challenge Laney faced was the negative opinion of many of his faculty about the building of the Presidential Parkway to the Carter Library and Center, after Laney had succeeded in recruiting the former US president to become a faculty member at Emory, with the hope that one day the Carter Center would be absorbed into the university. Another challenge of the era was apartheid in South Africa. Laney's missionary heart on this issue conflicted with his position as a director of the Coca-Cola Company and the university's heavy investment in Coca-Cola stock through its endowment portfolio. Finally, Laney and Emory were confronted with several painful racial challenges that called into question the university's commitment to racial equality. The Sabrina Collins case of 1990 receives particular attention.

Finally, the subject of chapter 6 will be Laney as moral leader, attempting to view Laney's work at Emory through the lens of leader, evaluating the strengths and limitations of his vision, his tolerance for ambiguity, his commitment to teamwork, his personal charisma, and his moral sagacity. These characteristics will be placed in the context of Max Weber's notion of positional authority, and they will be evaluated alongside some of the theories of leadership in higher education, such as those promoted by Michael Cohen and James March, and Estella Bensimon and Anna Neumann.[16] I conclude with the view that among Laney's most enduring legacies was his commitment that higher education as a fundamentally moral endeavor requires academic presidential leadership that is moral both in word and action. Once the detailed analysis of these six chapters is complete, we will have more insight into Emory's maturation as a leading research university, into the leadership given by Laney, and into the development of higher education in this country in the latter twentieth century.

As this work is biographical, I adhere to the biographical approaches espoused by the contributors to the volumes edited by Stephen Oates, Norman Denzin, and Craig Kridel.[17] These writers suggest that biography is a form of art, best done when the writing engages the reader's mind and heart. Biographies appeal to us, according to Oates, because we are naturally curious people. Writing about others offers us access to human experience.[18]

Most writers about biography caution that the writer be careful not to over-identify with her/his subject. Paul Kendall argues for as much impartiality as possible, while recognizing the empathy the writer will have for the subject.[19] This caution is particularly appropriate in my case. I have known of Laney for a great deal of my life. He has been a family friend since the mid-1960s when he taught at the Vanderbilt Divinity School, at the same time my father was on the faculty there. When I came to Emory as a student in 1983, he was president of Emory, and I had the opportunity to reconnect with him. While I never knew him in a social way, I did observe his work with interest, and met with him personally on one occasion to discuss a student matter.

I was an administrator at Emory for eight years before he announced his resignation. For five of those years, I worked somewhat closely with him on fund raising matters, relating to donor stewardship and solicitation. Now, as a college president myself, I find myself drawn to him even more. His leadership style, his position on certain issues, his articulation of and passion for the moral dimensions of a private liberal arts education have greatly influenced the leadership I bring to LaGrange College.[20] In the spring of 1997, at the time of my inauguration, he did me the honor of serving as the keynote speaker for that occasion. In 2000, Laney served as LaGrange's baccalaureate speaker, and was awarded the honorary doctor of divinity at that year's commencement. So, personal identification with Laney is natural for me. I have attempted, however, to be appropriately critical in my analysis of his leadership at Emory and to avoid having this work seem more hagiographical than historical and biographical.

Finally, it should be noted that Laney has permitted me use of his papers for this book and that Emory University has granted me permission to use the White, Bowden, Woodruff, and Laney Papers cited throughout this work, along with the photographs. Emory holds the copyright to all of these materials.

---

[1]Mary Ann Dzuback, *Robert M. Hutchins: Portrait of an Educator* (Chicago: University of Chicago Press, 1991); Richard Storr, *Harper's University: The Beginning* (Chicago: University of Chicago Press, 1966); Hugh Hawkins, *Between Harvard and America: The Educational Leadership of Charles W. Eliot* (New York: Oxford University Press, 1991); Wayne J. Urban, *Black Scholar: Horace Mann Bond 1904–1972* (Athens: University of Georgia Press, 1992).

[2]Laurence Veysey, *The Emergence of the American University* (Chicago: University of Chicago Press, 1965); Frederick Rudolph, *The American College and University: A History* (New York: Alfred A. Knopf, Inc., 1983).

[3]Marlene Ross and Madeleine F. Green, *The American College President: 1998 Edition* (Washington, DC: American Council on Education, 1998) 63–64.

[4]Andrew W.M. Bierle, "The Vision," *Emory Magazine* 69 (Winter 1994): 4–12.

[5]Bierle, "The Vision," 4–12.

[6]Billy E. Frye, "Introduction: Emory and the Crisis in American Higher Education," *Emory Report* 47 (26 September 1994): 2.

[7]Frye, "Emory and the Crisis," 9.

[8]Lamar Howard of Yale University told the University trustees at a 1987 retreat that "You're being talked about as a new Hopkins or a new Chicago, but I know that you plan to be a very different national university." See "Transcription of Remarks Presented at the Trustee Retreat, March 13–14, 1987," 13–14 March 1987, Laney Papers, box 10, folder "Trustees Retreat 1987," Special Collections Department, Robert W. Woodruff Library, Emory University Atlanta, 72. Hereafter, the location of all materials at the Robert W. Woodruff Library will be designated by the letters RWWL.

[9]James T. Laney, interview by author, tape recording, Emory University, Atlanta, 17 August 1998.

[10]Storr, *Harper's University*, 11–12. In regard to the prominence of Chicago, Storr writes, "...the city had more than trebled in size in two decades [1870–1890] and had become the second largest in the United States: the sheer presence of the rising city in the West partly explains the founding of the University." As for Atlanta, its prominence was seen, in part, by its selection to host the Democratic National Convention in 1988 and the Centennial Olympic Games in 1996.

[11]Benjamin McArthur, "A Gamble on Youth: Robert M. Hutchins, the University of Chicago and the Politics of Presidential Selection," *History of Education Quarterly* 30 (Summer 1990): 165.

[12]Dzuback, *Robert M. Hutchins*, 208–209.

[13]Laney describes himself as a four degree recipient of Yale. He earned the B.A., B.D. and Ph.D. (Christian Ethics), and in 1993 was awarded an honorary doctorate.

[14]Laney was on the faculty of the Vanderbilt Divinity School in the area of Christian Ethics from 1965 until 1969. He came to Emory in 1969 as dean of the Candler School of Theology, the post he held until his appointment as president in 1977.

[15]Emory was established as a university by the Methodist Episcopal Church, South, in 1915. To this day, Emory continues an affiliate status with the Southeastern Jurisdiction of the United Methodist Church.

[16]Michael D. Cohen and James G. March, "Leadership in an Organized Anarchy," in *Organization and Governance in Higher Education: An ASHE Reader* (Needham Heights MA: Ginn Press, 1991); Estella Bensimon and Anna Neumann, *Redesigning Collegiate Leadership: Teams and Teamwork in Higher Education* (Baltimore: Johns Hopkins University Press, 1993).

[17]Stephen Oates, ed., *Biography as High Adventure: Life-Writers Speak on Their Art* (Amherst: University of Massachusetts Press, 1986); Norman K. Denzin, *Interpretative Biography* (Newbury Park CA: SAGE Publications, Inc., 1989); Craig Kridel, ed., *Writing Educational Biography: Explorations in Qualitative Research* (New York: Garland Publishing, Inc., 1998).

[18]Oates, *Biography as High Adventure*, ix.

[19]Oates, *Biography as High Adventure*, 35.

[20]LaGrange College is a private, four-year, liberal arts institution, affiliated with the United Methodist Church. It is located in LaGrange, Georgia, and has a student enrollment of approximately 1,000. LaGrange College is the oldest private higher education institution in Georgia, having been founded in 1831.

CHAPTER ONE

LANEY'S RISE TO THE PRESIDENCY
OF EMORY UNIVERSITY

The selection of a new president is a crucial moment in the life of any institution of higher learning. The background of individuals selected as president is often as diverse as the number of persons who hold the position. Family histories, educational credentials, administrative experiences and institutional considerations are all important factors in candidate selection. Dynamics such as these were evident in the selection of Eliot at Harvard, Harper and Hutchins at Chicago, and Bond at Fort Valley. Hawkins explains that although Eliot was not a unanimous choice as the president of Harvard in 1869 he appealed to a majority of the overseers because of his youthfulness at thirty-five years of age and his scientific background in chemistry which spoke to the rise of original investigation, a hallmark of higher education in that era.[1] In 1892, Harper was chosen at the young age of thirty-four, having demonstrated, Storr contends, an aggressiveness and intellectual acumen that appealed especially to Rockefeller, who would finance most of Harper's empire building of the new university.[2] In 1929, Hutchins, too, was young at thirty years of age. According to McArthur, he was the compromise candidate after an exhaustive yearlong search, where the committee was split between whether the new president should promote teaching or research. Hutchins' lawyer background and administrative experience at Yale made him the satisfactory choice.[3] Urban explains that Bond in 1939, at thirty-five years of age, accepted the presidency of Fort Valley, after strong encouragement from Edwin Embree of the Rosenwald Fund, who intimated that the foundation would support the institution if he accepted.[4]

James T. Laney's selection as president of Emory University in 1977 differs from the selection of Eliot, Harper, Hutchins, and Bond in that he was older at forty-nine years of age, which was an age slightly below the average age of presidents of his era.[5] Despite the difference in age, the search at Emory that resulted in Laney's selection demonstrates institutional considerations and influences similar to the accessions of Eliot, Harper, Hutchins, and Bond.

When Laney was named president of Emory on 17 March 1977, this news to some observers was surprising. Observers inside and outside the Emory community did not believe it possible that an emerging private research university would appoint as its chief executive a theological dean and an ordained United Methodist clergyman.[6] Skeptics had two concerns. First, some board members worried that a clergyman and dean of a theology school would not have enough administrative acumen to guide a complex university. Second, some faculty worried that a clergyman and theological dean would neither understand fully nor operate successfully in an environment committed foremost to free inquiry and not to God. Skepticism toward clergy as presidents had been true of higher education since the early 1900s, when, Rudolph contends, clergy were seen generally "to lack skill in the way of the world, because [their] commitment to classical curriculum stood in the way of more practical and popular emphasis."[7]

Although Emory had its roots firmly planted in the soil of the Methodist Church,[8] Laney's most immediate predecessors—with the exception of the first university president, Bishop Warren A. Candler—had non-theological backgrounds. Candler had chaired the committee of the Methodist Episcopal Church, South, that formalized Emory's move to university status and its physical move from Oxford, Georgia, to

Atlanta, Georgia. He was also a former president of Emory College, a post he held from 1888 until his election as bishop in 1898.[9]

As early as 1920, when Bishop Candler stepped down as the chief executive, the university demonstrated its comfort with a non-clergyman as president by appointing to the helm Harvey Cox, a philosopher, Harvard Ph.D., and active Methodist Episcopal Church, South, layman. Cox's success as Emory's president for over two decades, as well as his ability to maintain a church connection as an active layman, led subsequent search committees to give priority to the academic credentials of his successors, with the expectation that the church tie could be satisfied with membership in the denomination.

Following President Cox were Presidents Goodrich White (1943–1957)—a psychologist and University of Chicago Ph.D.—and Walter Martin (1957–1962)—a Southern historian and University of North Carolina, Chapel Hill, Ph.D. Both had prior significant administrative experience in higher education and were active laymen in the Methodist Church.[10] In the search that resulted in the selection of Walter Martin, the faculty believed that the office should be held by a Christian. The faculty senate in its "Report to the Trustees Committee on the Selection of a President for the University" wrote as their "utmost consideration that the president-to-be of Emory University be dedicated wholeheartedly to the Christian interpretation of God and Man as manifested in Jesus Christ, this being the basis of Christian Education."[11] The document, however, said nothing about the person's being ordained, although those close to the search remember that the expectation was that the eventual selectee be a member of the Methodist Church.[12]

By 1963, the university seemed content to secure the best credentialed person possible for the presidency without regard to church affiliation. Sanford Atwood, the then-provost at Cornell University, was tapped for the top job. His academic credentials were stellar. He was a geneticist, with a Ph.D. from the University of Wisconsin. His church affiliation was Presbyterian. For the sake of appearances, however, Atwood is said to have consented to an unwritten agreement with the board of trustees that if offered the position, he would join the Glenn Memorial Methodist Church on the Emory campus.[13] Membership records do not show that he ever did this, and some Emory graduates and friends, including Henry Bowden, the then-chairman of the Emory board of trustees, were disappointed that he did not take an active role in a church.[14] Despite the concerns about church involvement on the part of the president, Emory had clearly developed a precedent for hiring non-clergy as presidents by the time the search for Atwood's successor was begun in 1976. That Dr. James T. Laney—the dean of the Candler School of Theology, professor of Christian Ethics, and a United Methodist clergyman—should be chosen as president seemed unusual, if not contrary to established practice.

While the Emory practice of hiring non-clergy presidents seemed inimical to Laney's selection as president, his personal and professional background was rich and varied enough to make him a suitable, albeit uncommon, choice. Born in 1927 in Arkansas, Laney was the only child of Thomas Mann and Mary Hughey Laney. His relationship to his mother was close, but Laney remembers a distant and aloof relationship with his car salesman father. Still, the church played an important role in the family's life, and Sunday attendance was assumed. In many respects, Laney's childhood church and work-related experiences, including his work at Emory, were attempts to gain the fatherly approval and affirmation he missed as a child.[15]

Laney's love of learning and understanding of the importance of education were encouraged at an early age by his maternal grandparents, James M. and Hattie Mae Hughey. Laney spent many summers on their Arkansas farm. His grandfather was a learned man and an ordained Methodist minister. He graduated from Hendrix College and received a bachelor of divinity from Vanderbilt University in the 1890s. Laney remembers that his grandfather would read the Greek New Testament each day, in addition to reading with Laney the encyclopedia series *The Book of Knowledge*. His grandparents were pious and formal—referring to each other as Mr. and Mrs. Hughey—and demonstrated to each other and those they knew a love and care that had a critical impact on Laney.[16]

Beginning in the fifth grade, Laney showed his entrepreneurial spirit when he worked at odd jobs, including drug store clerk and grocery store clerk. In each position, he thrived on the challenge of the work and on seeing tasks through to completion. The approval of his bosses and the opportunity for increased responsibility with new tasks were his reward. Laney especially remembers at fifteen years of age being asked that summer to manage a gas station, including three employees, after the owner had been drafted into World War II. Saturdays were the busiest day of the week, as each gas station competed to wash the most cars. Not to be outdone, Laney would walk the downtown area of the small Arkansas community where he worked, asking people if he could wash their car, taking the keys, driving the car to the station, and returning the clean car to its owner. Such was the drive Laney showed early on in life to compete and succeed.

After graduation in 1945 as one of four co-valedictorians from Central High School in Memphis, Laney enrolled to study economics at Yale University as a Southern Regional Scholar, which was a scholarship designed to bring to Yale promising Southern students.[17] His Yale experience was interrupted by being drafted into the Counter Intelligence Unit of the US Army, where he was assigned to Korea, a culture he had never before experienced. While there he found himself drawn to the people, who were overcoming enormous economic and political challenges. The tour in Korea influenced him in many ways, giving him lifelong friends, a deep love and appreciation for the culture and language, and a desire to return someday, perhaps as a missionary. Eventually, he would learn to speak Korean fluently.

After his World War II duty, Laney returned to Yale, where he grad-uated with a B.A. in economics in 1950. In his last years at Yale, Laney encountered a young, assistant professor of English, Dr. Martin Price,[18] in a survey of English literature. This professor and his course sparked a love of nineteenth-century literature that remains with Laney to this day. Laney was especially attracted to Price's grasp and mastery of the materi-al. He taught Laney how to read thoughtfully and critically works such as *Paradise Lost*, *Vanity Fair*, and the writings of Shakespeare. Laney remembers that Price focused on the profound moral dimensions of life addressed by the writings, developing in Laney an intellectual concern for individual character and moral agency.[19]

Laney's relationship to Price was complemented by a meaningful friendship that he developed with the Reverend Doug Cook, the director of Yale's Wesley Foundation, who over the years would remain Laney's closest friend until Cook's death in 1997. Laney described Cook as hav-ing a "winsome Christian spirit," while living on the verge of poverty—although never seeming to sacrifice—in a culture of excessive drive and ambition. No doubt, Cook was for Laney an alter ego. While greatly driven and very ambitious himself, Laney found appealing in Cook the depth of Christian conviction that would permit him to have less power materially and socially.[20]

Despite Laney's economics major, his upbringing in a family com-mitted to the church, his experience in Korea, and the relationships he developed with Price and Cook at Yale compelled him to commit him-self to a lifetime of Christian service by seeking ordination in the Methodist Church. He was encouraged in this choice by his new wife, the former Berta Radford, niece of Admiral William Radford, chairman of the Joint Chiefs of Staff under President Dwight Eisenhower. Laney and Miss Radford married in 1949.

As a prerequisite to ordination, Laney had to secure a bachelor of divinity degree. Arguably, the finest place to receive a theological education in the early 1950s was the Yale Divinity School, which had on its faculty some of the leading theologians of the century, including H. Richard Niebuhr. Of those who graduated from the college at Yale in 1950, ten enrolled that fall in the Yale Divinity School.[21]

For Laney, his graduate level theological study was an extension of his liberal arts education from Yale College, instilling in him a firm commitment to the importance of liberal arts study that would be a hallmark of his leadership at Emory. While in the divinity school, he became a disciple of Niebuhr, taking every course he offered, including Ph.D.-level seminars. Laney was awed by the intellectual capacity of Niebuhr, who began each class with a handwritten prayer, symbolizing, for Laney, his subservience to God. Like Laney's grandfather, Niebuhr, according to Laney, demonstrated to students an unostentatious piety, based on a deep faith. Niebuhr's class lectures also demonstrated his struggle with issues of faith and morality in the world. Not until later did Laney learn that some of the class lectures he was hearing were the manuscript for Niebuhr's highly regarded work, *The Responsible Self.* Niebuhr's pious lifestyle and his encouragement to students to assist him in working through major theological issues had significant impact on Laney. Having Niebuhr as mentor also influenced his thinking about the role faculty should play in a liberal arts college.[22]

While in divinity school from 1950 until 1954, Laney held a number of positions, including student pastor of a church in Connecticut, and chaplain at the Choate School, where he taught courses in religion. He also was an instructor in several classes at Yale during his last year. Laney was flattered to be asked by Niebuhr to remain at Yale and work on his Ph.D. and to assist him with research projects, but Laney felt compelled to serve a church full time, all as preparation to return to Korea as a missionary. Thus, in 1955, after graduation from Yale Divinity School, Laney moved to Cincinnati, Ohio, where he became the pastor of St. Paul Methodist Church. While there he helped invigorate a dying congregation with an increase in membership and commitment. After three years, though, he accepted an assignment through the board of missions of the Methodist Church to become a missionary to Korea.[23]

Laney's task while in Korea was to give leadership to the Korean Student Christian Council, exposing him to a number of higher education institutions. He developed a close tie to Yonsei University, where he was eventually made associate professor of religion. Through his work, Laney became fast friends with student leaders, who eventually emerged as political leaders in Korea, and who were instrumental in lobbying US President William Clinton in 1993 for Laney's appointment as US Ambassador to Korea, a post he would hold for just over three years (1993–1997).[24]

The teaching opportunities Laney had at Yale and at Yonsei made him aware that he wanted to pursue teaching as a profession. To do this would require entry to a doctoral program, and after five years of missionary work, he decided to return to full-time study. Although admitted to the Ph.D. program at Cambridge University, Laney opted for the program in Christian Ethics at Yale. The Yale program he viewed as "more efficient," given that Yale was willing to work with him on minimizing the requirements for the degree. By this time, Laney and his wife had five children. The prospect of being a full-time student overseas, after having been away from this country for five years, was daunting, and, thus, Yale seemed the logical choice for his doctoral work.[25]

Laney thrived once again in the educational environment of Yale. By this time, Niebuhr had died, but the quality of the faculty was still stellar. Laney focused his energies on the popular topic of contextual ethics and on this subject wrote his dissertation, analyzing the structural and normative ethical approaches advanced by Karl Barth, Dietrich Bonhoeffer, and Paul Lehman. As part of his program, he read numerous speeches of turn-of-the-twentieth-century New England higher education presidents.[26] These speeches would greatly influence Laney later in the leadership he would bring to Emory.[27]

After graduation in 1966, he quickly secured employment at Vanderbilt University, where he served as assistant professor of Christian Ethics and director of Methodist Studies. He also served as pastor of the Pegram Methodist Church, a responsibility he shared with a Korean pastor. In 1968, William R. Cannon was elected to the episcopacy of the United Methodist Church, while serving as the dean of the Candler School of Theology at Emory, a post he had held since 1953. In looking for Cannon's successor, search committee members at Candler were committed to securing a youthful academic with administrative and pastoral experience.[28] When the committee found Laney at Vanderbilt, his appointment to Candler seemed propitious. So, in 1969, Laney came to Emory as dean of the Candler School of Theology and professor of Christian Ethics.

Soon after his arrival at Candler, Laney negotiated with Emory President Sanford Atwood that Candler be treated as a "tub on its own bottom." In exchange for seeking no subvention from the university, Candler would be permitted to keep all the money it raised. This was contrary to the practice of the other Emory professional schools which depended greatly on the university's largesse to function. Laney knew that the changes he felt were necessary at Candler would require an independence from university resources. Thus, he began to cut the budget and to raise money such that, in a brief time, Candler had an impressive reserve.[29]

In 1974, Laney took a one-half year sabbatical during the fall as a visiting professor at Harvard Divinity School. While there, it became apparent that Harvard had more in mind than just teaching when it made the offer to him to become a visiting faculty member. The leaders of Harvard were interested in preparing Laney for an offer to become the dean of the Harvard Divinity School. Although no firm offer was made,

Laney shared this information with Henry Bowden, chairman of the Emory board of trustees, when he returned to Emory that October to attend the fall meeting of the board of trustees. Bowden counseled Laney not to take Harvard seriously, for, as Bowden explained, he and other trustees had their eyes on Laney as a possible successor to Atwood, whenever he should step down. Since Laney had always assumed that Emory would never consider a theological dean as its president, this conversation was the first time he entertained the idea of becoming president of Emory. Laney returned to Candler following his sabbatical, and resumed the deanship.[30]

In 1975, President Atwood informed the board of trustees he was giving two year's notice before his retirement. He set as his retirement date 31 August 1977. Between Atwood's announcement of his retirement and Laney's selection as his successor, there were three developments that made Laney's appointment as president probable. The first occurrence was Laney's meeting and developing a relationship with Robert W. Woodruff, unarguably the most influential man in Atlanta and Emory's greatest benefactor. Woodruff was the chairman and chief executive officer of the Coca-Cola Company, a position he had held since 1923. Through his influence, he had made Coca-Cola one of the best-known product names in the world. His influence in Atlanta was considerable, as, for instance, he was credited with preventing riots during the funeral services for Dr. Martin Luther King, Jr., in Atlanta, by offering to cover all the expenses necessary to provide adequate security for the city. He also became a legendary "anonymous" benefactor to numerous Atlanta charities and cultural entities, such as the Boys' and Girls' Club, and the Atlanta Symphony Orchestra.[31]

Among Woodruff's closest friends was his personal physician, Garland Herndon, who was also vice president for health affairs at Emory. Herndon and Laney were neighbors, and had become friends sharing their views about Emory and higher education generally. At a social event in 1975 attended by Herndon, Laney and Woodruff had their first meeting. During that conversation, Woodruff invited Laney to visit his home. Laney accepted his offer, and this began a friendship that eventually developed into a meaningful spiritual relationship. While Herndon was Woodruff's personal physician, Laney became his personal chaplain.

Soon after the official presidential search was announced, Woodruff wrote the following letter to Bowden, who was serving as chairman of the search committee:

> Dear Henry:
>
> Having in mind the effort now underway to select a successor to Dr. Atwood, I would like to express for the consideration of your Search Committee the thought that it may be timely to recommend a successor from the current leadership of the University. It is the general practice of business corporations, of course, to promote from within their own organizations when a qualified candidate for a higher position is identifiable. The advantages of this procedure are obvious.
>
> Accordingly, I suggest the appointment of Dr. James T. Laney as Dr. Atwood's successor.... His attainments both before and since coming to Emory are impressive and I hope you will acquaint yourself with his truly out-standing record.
>
> Because your personal relationship with Dr. Laney is closer than mine, and if you agree that this thought is opportune, I hope it may also have your endorsement as you continue the process of choosing a president.[32]

Whether Woodruff's endorsement of Laney sealed his selection as president can never be fully known, but there is no doubt that Woodruff's recommendation was taken very seriously. Woodruff's endorsement of Laney's candidacy also mirrored the experience of other university presidents who received strong endorsement from significant contributors. Embree of the Rosenwald Fund had considerable influence in the selection of Hutchins at Chicago[33] and of Bond at Fort Valley.[34] Rockefeller, of course, supported the candidacy of Harper at Chicago.[35]

A second development that made Laney's selection as president of Emory likely was his efforts in 1975–1976 to secure the Hartford Theological Library collection for the Pitts Theology Library at Emory. A long-standing seminary in Hartford, Connecticut, the trustees of Hartford Seminary in 1972 decided that to be more competitive it was necessary to change radically the mission of the institution from a degree granting seminary, training pastors of the church, to a non-degree granting, continuing education program for those already in the clergy. This shift in mission compelled the trustees to sell its library of nearly 240,000 volumes, a collection that contained books written mostly prior to 1920.

Channing Jeschke, the director of the Pitts Theology Library at the time, persuaded Laney that the purchase of this library would be a coup for Candler and Emory, more than doubling the size of the Pitts Theology Library. As the Pitts Library was started soon after the founding of Candler School of Theology in 1914, Jeschke calculated that there would be little overlap in the collection. Laney was easily convinced, and he began making contact with officials at Hartford about the purchase, although he had no idea how to pay for it.[36]

In his initial contacts with officials at Hartford, Laney learned that the purchase price had been set at $1.25 million. Laney took this information with him to President Atwood, who was supportive, but insisted that Laney had to secure board approval because of the large price tag. In his meetings with the executive committee of the board, members began to see in Laney a determination and drive, as well as a vision, that they admired. Thus, they gave their blessing to the purchase, with the understanding that Laney had to secure the necessary funds.[37]

When Laney returned to Hartford with the offer, he learned that Billy Graham had already made an offer of $2 million. Graham's intent was to keep those items of the collection valuable to his ministry and sell the remainder. Hartford officials shared with Laney that they preferred that the collection remain intact and be housed in a seminary. They were interested in Emory's offer, but insisted that the purchase price would now have to be no less than $1.75 million.[38]

Once again Laney had to return to the Emory board to secure its blessing for a $500,000 increase in the offer, which he received, but not without skepticism on the part of some board members about whether Laney truly knew what he was doing.[39] With some effort, Laney was successful in securing the necessary funding for the purchase from the likes of Stanley Kresge, the Mellon Foundation, and Miss Margaret Pitts of Waverly Hall, Georgia,[40] and the Hartford collection was secured for Emory. Overnight, the Pitts Theology Library became the second largest theological library in North America, trailing only Union Theological Library in New York. News of the purchase gained national attention. A full page article ran in the *New York Times* about the purchase and the move of the collection by truck caravan, in what amounted to four and one-half miles of shelf space. The article had this to say about the purchase: "The acquisition by Emory gives its seminary, the Candler School of Theology, an immediate increase in prestige and affords the South its first major center for historical theological research."[41] For the first time, Emory, through its theology school, was getting national publicity, and the library was among the finest to be found anywhere.

A third development that led to Laney's probable selection was the publication of an article titled "The Reputation of American Professional Schools" in *Change Magazine* in 1975. It ranked Emory's Candler School of Theology as the sixth best theological institution in North America, behind Harvard, Yale, University of Chicago, Princeton Theological Seminary, and Union Theological Seminary of New York.[42] For the first time, Emory received recognition for having a top ten nationally ranked school. Never before had Emory had any of its schools ranked in the top twenty-five nationally. Although the universe of theology schools was smaller than that of other professional schools, this did not change the fact that Emory could tout itself as having a nationally ranked program.[43]

The Woodruff endorsement, the Hartford Library acquisition, and the boost in rankings made Laney a very attractive candidate to succeed Atwood. In addition, some trustees welcomed restoring the presidency to an academic and clergyman of the United Methodist Church.[44] Still, Laney's selection was not guaranteed. Concerns of some trustees and faculty had to be overcome. The skepticism of some board members about the change of purchase price in the Hartford Collection led them to wonder if a theological dean could adequately handle the budgetary demands of a complex institution such as Emory. Furthermore, although the board valued the relationship of the university to the United Methodist Church, some members were comfortable with the historic precedent they had set in hiring non-clergy and non-United Methodists as president. If anything, for some trustees, Laney's ordination in the United Methodist Church was a strike against him.[45] Even the board document used to entice prospective candidates to the position had little to say about the expectations of the new president and her/his church affiliation. The only reference to the church was this: "they [prospective candidates] must relate effectively to the varied constituencies of the University, including the United Methodist Church."[46]

In an effort to dispel any notion among the trustees that Laney was not up to the task of serving as chief executive, board members partial to Laney wrote letters to Bowden extolling his virtues. One especially strongly worded letter came from trustee D. W. Brooks,[47] who served also as chairman of Candler's Committee of 100—a fund raising group—and who knew Laney and his abilities well. In his letter to Bowden, he wrote:

> When you look at Dean Laney's training, it is about as perfect as you could possibly have. The fact that he was a brilliant student first in economics graduating cum laude [Yale University] and then going back later into the ministry, I don't think you could have a person with a better background. Business people on the Committee, of course, should recognize this training, which is excellent for a person who is going to have the responsibility for a university.[48]

Brooks' letter and the letter from Woodruff to Bowden indicate that very influential Atlanta leaders were trying to settle the matter in favor of Laney.

Even more challenging than the few board members who had doubts about Laney was the desire of Emory faculty members to assert their collective authority and assure for themselves a voice, and preferably a vote, in the selection of their new leader. This was a practice well-established at Chicago by the time of the search for Hutchins, and in most private higher education institutions by 1981.[49] With the exception of the Atwood search, which permitted two faculty members to be "consultants" to the search committee, no faculty had ever been involved in the selection of an Emory chief executive. According to Dr. Judson Ward, Emory vice president for academic affairs during the Atwood administration, the faculty "consultants" in the Atwood search were hand-selected for their known willingness to acquiesce to anyone the board might want. Thus, they were little more than "yes-men."[50] For the search for Atwood's successor, the faculty wanted to make sure they were taken more seriously in the process.

While Atwood had given two years' notice of his intent to retire, Bowden decided to delay the beginning of the search for at least one year, so as not to make Atwood a lame duck.[51] It was impossible, though, to keep news of Atwood's decision private, and word began to circulate among faculty about the prospects for the search. Thus, soon after Atwood's announcement, two faculty members, representing the Emory Unit of the American Association of University Professors (AAUP), wrote to Bowden urging the involvement of faculty in the selection process.[52] They enclosed with their letter two AAUP-related documents— "Statement on the Governance of Colleges and Universities" and "Faculty Participation in the Selection and Retention of Administrators." Both documents called for greater faculty involvement in the governance of the institution, including allowing faculty to have voice and vote in the selection of presidents. Bowden's response was prompt and defended the trustees' right to make the decision exclusively. He wrote: "It must, of course, always be understood that though we [the trustees] encourage and need help in regard to the selection of a President, in the final analysis the duty devolves upon the Trustees and the responsibility for failure must be theirs also. Under such circumstances, there can be no delegation of such authority."[53]

Bowden believed faculty involvement in the search was a closed matter until he received word in late March 1976 that the Faculty Advisory Council of the University Senate, in a highly unusual move, voted "to urge the Trustees to appoint representative faculty of the University as voting members of the Search Committee for the selection of a new University President."[54] Bowden agreed to a meeting with a select group of the Faculty Advisory Council. He presented his views on the matter, and they hashed out a compromise whereby it was agreed that a five member Faculty Advisory Committee, selected by the University Senate, would be granted permission to review candidate files, interview candidates, and make recommendations to the board.[55]

By this time, faculty knew of Laney's candidacy and the support he had from some trustees. According to Theodore Weber, who headed the Faculty Advisory Committee, the committee worried that the search would be seen as a sham if external candidates were not courted and brought to campus. Weber was in a position of having to relate this to Bowden when they met in late October 1976. In this meeting, Bowden indicated that it was the desire of the search committee to name Laney then as president so that he could begin to help set budget and make a smooth transition with Atwood. Weber succeeded in persuading Bowden to do otherwise, arguing that it was critical that faculty be given a chance to see candidates from outside the university.[56]

Bowden named himself chairman of the search committee. Seven other members were appointed.[57] James Sibley, Woodruff's appointee to the board a few years earlier, was placed on the search committee several months after the committee had been named, perhaps, Sibley believes, to be certain that Woodruff's preference for Laney be represented in the deliberations of the committee.[58] Over the course of the six months the search was conducted, the search committee received 123 applications and invited six persons for interviews.[59]

The search for Atwood's successor produced at least one attractive alternative to Laney's candidacy. Frank Rhodes of the University of Michigan was interviewed on 10–11 January 1976 and impressed all groups with which he met. He was clearly the top choice of the Faculty Advisory Committee,[60] and became the top choice of the search committee as well.[61] They were all surprised when they learned through the 17 February 1977 issue of the *New York Times* that he had been offered and had accepted the presidency of Cornell University. In this article, Rhodes revealed that he was a finalist for the Emory presidency and had declined offers from four other institutions.[62] On 25 February, Klein and

Weber for the faculty committee wrote to Bowden urging that other names be solicited, but the request was ignored.[63]

With Rhodes out of the picture, the search was settled in favor of Laney. Faculty, according to Weber, were resigned to accept the Laney appointment.[64] That the search committee included only trustees meant that the tension and division within the committee that existed in 1929 in the search for Hutchins at Chicago, where five trustees and five faculty served, was avoided.[65] Thus, Laney was selected president without dissent by the trustees on 17 March 1977.[66]

Although the odds may have made the appointment of a theological dean and clergyman to the presidency of Emory highly unlikely, Laney's background, and especially his accomplishments while dean at Candler and his relationship to influential Atlanta leaders, such as Woodruff and Brooks, made his selection palatable to trustees and faculty. His upbringing as a child, his educational experience at Yale, his relationship to the church, and his administrative experience in higher education would all combine to make his sixteen year presidency at Emory a significant era of growth and change for the institution.

---

[1]Hugh Hawkins, *Between Harvard and America: The Educational Leadership of Charles W. Eliot* (New York: Oxford University Press, 1991) 44–46. Eliot was elected by a vote of sixteen to eight.

[2]Richard Storr, *Harper's University: The Beginning* (Chicago: University of Chicago Press, 1966) 27.

[3]Benjamin McArthur, "A Gamble on Youth: Robert M. Hutchins, the University of Chicago and the Politics of Presidential Selection," *History of Education Quarterly* 30 (Summer 1990): 165.

[4]Wayne J. Urban, *Black Scholar: Horace Mann Bond 1904–1972* (Athens: University of Georgia Press, 1992) 71–72.

[5]Marlene Ross and Madeleine F. Green, *The American College President: 1998 Edition* (Washington, DC: American Council on Education, 1998) 106. Their

study shows that in 1986 the median and mean ages for presidents of independent doctorate-granting institutions were 56 and 55.9 respectively.

[6]James T. Laney, interview by author, tape recording, Emory University, Atlanta, 23 June 1998.

[7]Frederick Rudolph, *The American College and University: A History* (New York: Alfred A. Knopf, Inc., 1983) 419.

[8]Emory was founded by the denomination in Oxford, Georgia, in 1836 and established as a university in 1915.

[9]Bishop Candler held the title of chancellor. There was no president per se.

[10]In 1939, the Methodist Episcopal Church, South, joined with two other denominations to form the Methodist Church. In 1968, the Methodist Church and the Evangelical United Brethren Church joined to form the United Methodist Church.

[11]"Report to the Trustees Committee for the Selection of a President for the University," May 1956, Goodrich C. White Papers, series I, box 18, RWWL.

[12]Henry Bowden, interview by author, tape recording, Emory University, Atlanta, 2 March 1995; Judson Ward, interview by author, tape recording, Emory University, Atlanta, 10 March 1995.

[13]Bowden interview.

[14]Bowden interview.

[15]Laney interview, 23 June 1998. Later in life, according to Laney, his father showed more interest in his pursuits, including a close and loving relationship with his (Laney's) five children.

[16]Laney interview, 23 June 1998.

[17]James T. Laney, interview by author, tape recording, Emory University, Atlanta, 17 August 1998.

[18]Price later became a Sterling Professor of English, the highest faculty appointment one can receive at Yale.

[19]Laney interview, 23 June 1998.

[20]Laney interview, 23 June 1998.

[21]Laney interview, 23 June 1998.

[22]Laney interview, 23 June 1998.

[23]Laney interview, 23 June 1998.

[24]Laney interview, 23 June 1998.

[25]Laney interview, 23 June 1998.

[26]As an example of these speeches, the reader is referred to the following: Thomas Edward Frank, "Conserving a Rational World: Theology, Ethics, and the Nineteenth Century American Ideal" (Ph.D. diss., Emory University, 1981). In this work, Frank focuses on the speeches of three turn-of-the-century college presidents:

William Jewett Tucker of Dartmouth (1893–1909), William DeWitt Hyde of Bowdoin (1885–1917), and Henry Churchill King of Oberlin (1903–1927). Each of these presidents, according to Frank, was influenced in his thinking about higher education by the nineteenth-century rational and moral synthesis, which encouraged a college ideal of shaping the character and moral development of students. Laney served as an advisor to this dissertation.

[27]Laney interview, 17 August 1998.

[28]Ward interview.

[29]Laney interviews, 23 June 1998 and 17 August 1998. Laney's recollection is that in the year prior to his arrival Candler received in excess of $500,000 from the university to cover the deficit. Growing support from the United Methodist Church in excess of $1 million per year through the Ministerial Education Fund and a growing enrollment gave Laney confidence that Candler could succeed financially, independent of the university.

[30]Laney interviews, 23 June 1998 and 17 August 1998.

[31]For a review of Woodruff's charitable interests see Woodruff Papers, RWWL.

[32]Robert W. Woodruff to Henry L. Bowden, 5 October 1976, Robert W. Woodruff Alpha Files, box 34, folder 13, RWWL.

[33]Mary Ann Dzuback, *Robert M. Hutchins: Portrait of an Educator* (Chicago: University of Chicago Press, 1991) 75; McArthur, "A Gamble on Youth," 174. Dzuback indicates that Embree wrote to the search committee that he found appealing in Hutchins his "creative ideas, strong leadership and unconventional brilliance." Both Dzuback and McArthur note that George Vincent, president of the Rockefeller Foundation, was also key in encouraging Hutchins' selection.

[34]Urban, *Black Scholar*, 71.

[35]Storr, *Harper's University*, 27.

[36]Laney interview, 23 June 1998.

[37]Bowden interview.

[38]Laney interview, 23 June 1998.

[39]Bowden interview; Laney interview, 23 June 1998. Board member George Craft was especially vocal in his skepticism, according to Laney. Bowden remembers that some of this skepticism had to be addressed in the early stages of the presidential search, about which more will be said later in this chapter.

[40]James T. Laney, interview by author, tape recording, Emory University, Atlanta, 11 November 1997.

[41]Kenneth A. Briggs, "Prized Theological Library Sold to Emory U. for $1.75 Million," *New York Times*, 21 August 1976, 23.

[42]Peter M. Blau and Rebecca Zames Margulies, "The Reputation of American Professional Schools," *Change Magazine* 6 (Winter 1974–1975): 45. Candler was

tied for sixth place with Claremont Graduate School and Southern Methodist University.

[43]Laney interview, 23 June 1998.

[44]Bowden interview.

[45]Ibid.

[46]"Guidelines for the Selection of Emory University's President," May 1976, Bowden Papers, RWWL.

[47]Brooks was founder and chief executive officer of Goldkist, and an internationally recognized figure in agriculture. He served as advisor to seven US presidents on agricultural matters. His influence in Atlanta and throughout the nation at the time was considerable.

[48]D. W. Brooks to Henry Bowden, 22 October 1976, Bowden Papers, RWWL.

[49]McArthur, "A Gamble on Youth," 165. Also see Judith Black McLaughlin, "From Secrecy to Sunshine: An Overview of Presidential Search Practice," *Research in Higher Education* 22/2 (1985): 198. In 1981, McLaughlin conducted a study on the presidential search processes used in higher education institutions that year. She found that of twenty-nine private higher education institutions, only four committees were made up exclusively of trustees. In most cases, trustees comprised less than one-half of the committee. Six committees had more than one-half trustees. Four committees had an equal number of trustees and non-trustees. Fourteen committees had fewer than one-half trustees. Her study does not indicate the exact number of faculty who served on these committees, except to say that faculty served on every committee with the exception of the four committees comprised of trustees exclusively.

[50]Ward interview.

[51]Bowden interview.

[52]Gene Tucker and Albert Stone to Henry Bowden, 11 November 1975, Bowden Papers, RWWL.

[53]Henry Bowden to Gene Tucker and Albert Stone, 13 November 1975, Bowden Papers, RWWL.

[54]Jake Ward to Henry Bowden, 31 March 1976, Bowden Papers, RWWL.

[55]Jake Ward Memo to Emory community, Ted Weber Papers, 17 May 1976. Members of the Faculty Advisory Committee were Carole Hahn (Educational Studies), Luella Klein (Grady Hospital), Gerald Kock (Law School), Henry Sharp (Mathematics), and Ted Weber (Theology). Alumni and Student Committees were also formed, but they played a much lesser role in the process.

[56]Dr. Theodore Weber, interview by author, note recording, Emory University, Atlanta, 1 March 1995.

[57]The other trustees on the search committee were Bishop William R. Cannon, George Craft, Howard Dobbs, Mary Lynn Morgan, Erle Phillips, and Pollard Turman. See "Presidential Selection Committee," 1976, Bowden Papers, RWWL.

[58]James Sibley, interview by author, note recording, Atlanta, 14 July 1998. Sibley remembers that when he would visit in Woodruff's home in the late afternoons, Woodruff would quiz him about why the trustees had not yet named Laney president.

[59]Jake Ward to Henry Bowden, 18 January 1977, Bowden Papers, RWWL.

[60]Ted Weber to Henry Bowden, 3 February 1977, Bowden Papers, RWWL.

[61]William R. Cannon, *A Magnificent Obsession: The Autobiography of William Ragsdale Cannon* (Nashville: Abingdon Press, 1999) 279–80.

[62]Judith Cummings, "New President is Elected at Cornell," *New York Times*, 17 February 1977, 34.

[63]Luella Klein and Theodore Weber to Henry Bowden, 25 February 1977, Bowden Papers, RWWL.

[64]Luella Klein and Theodore Weber to Henry Bowden, 25 February 1977, Bowden Papers. Weber noted that some faculty believed that Bowden did not respond quickly enough to the news that Rhodes had been offered the job at Cornell by trying to convince him to come to Emory. Weber acknowledged, though, that the Cornell post was more attractive than Emory's in 1977, and that it would have been difficult to make a convincing case for Emory.

[65]McArthur, "A Gamble on Youth," 165.

[66]Emory University Board of Trustee minutes, 17 March 1977, RWWL. Laney says he does not have much recollection of the search. He claims to have been protected from the behind-the-scenes politics of the process. He says he does remember that soon after his selection Bowden commented to him that he (Bowden) "sure had a difficult time with Ted Weber in the search." (From Laney interview, 23 June 1998.)

CHAPTER TWO

LANEY THE COMMUNICATOR
ON EDUCATION AS A MORAL ENDEAVOR

Perhaps the most demanding, and most important, activity of any college president is that of speech making and writing. Through these media, presidents convey their vision about the purpose of the institution and seek to gain support for that vision from the institution's many constituents. Hawkins notes that both during and following Eliot's presidency, Eliot made public presentations almost daily about Harvard and his commitment to the "system of liberty" in a liberal arts education. His skill at speaking and his public statements were highly prized by the media who, according to Hawkins, sought out Eliot for a statement, if he did not offer one on the issue of the day.[1] Dzuback relates how Hutchins spoke masterfully during his time as president of the University of Chicago. While Hutchins never fully convinced all of his critics about his desire for a general education curriculum at Chicago, he was persistent and persuasive enough to garner support for the implementation of the program, even though the program did not survive after his departure. Dzuback notes, however, that Hutchins is probably best remembered for his elegant, articulate, compassionate, and convincing oratory.[2] While the vision of Eliot and Hutchins, and their noted oratorical abilities, helped ingratiate them with the various constituents of their institutions even when problems would arise, Bond's success at conveying his vision met with more limited success. Urban notes that, while at Fort Valley, Bond was "a respected spokesman" for the college. Yet, his success at Lincoln was much more limited, confronted as he was with challenges by the alumni about athletics and by alumni and funders about the school's slowness in attracting white students. Bond never seemed to develop and express a compelling vision for Lincoln that enabled him to overcome these challenges.[3]

No less than Eliot and Hutchins, Laney proved himself to be an expert and persuasive communicator of his vision for a liberal arts education. Also, he was more successful than Hutchins in making the implementation of this vision an enduring legacy of his presidency. To understand fully the development of Emory during the Laney years, it is important to know something of Laney's vision for a liberal arts education, which he articulated repeatedly throughout his sixteen-year tenure. Through lectures, baccalaureate, convocation, and commencement addresses given at Emory and institutions around the world, Laney articulated a vision for the liberal arts that moved beyond giving students credentials for a career, to giving students character and moral development intended to make them effective and contributing citizens of society. He also said often that the academic president is a moral leader.

Laney took the public role of his presidency very seriously, as can be seen from the numerous speeches he gave and articles he wrote while in office. His archival files and published writings indicate that in his sixteen years in office, Laney published forty-one articles. The majority of these articles—approximately thirty and most of them published in Emory's alumni magazine—were taken from speeches he gave at baccalaureate services, commencements, official church assemblies, and academic gatherings, such as the Society for Values in Higher Education, the Association of American Colleges (now the Association of American Colleges and Universities), and the National Association for Independent Colleges and Universities. Approximately ten of the articles he published were in refereed journals.[4]

Cultural Analysis that Influenced Laney's View of a Liberal Arts Education

In every generation, university presidents are confronted with a cultural environment that influences how they approach the mission of the institution. How well presidents understand and articulate the issues of the era determines in large measure the success of their presidencies. The growth of graduate and professional education in the late 1800s led to the emphasis that Eliot placed on research and the elective system at Harvard.[5] Hutchins was confronted with the Great Depression and the Red Scare. The Red Scare threatened the very foundations of academic freedom, and Hutchins became a leading and nationally recognized proponent of academic freedom by shielding his faculty from outside interference.[6] Aside from these issues, Dzuback notes that Hutchins' "homiletic talents were most inspirational when he spoke of the materialism of American society, the moral laxity of businessmen and politicians, and the problem of placing means before ends in much of human activity." The passion he displayed in these presentations kept him in the students' good graces throughout his tenure at Chicago.[7] Bond faced the challenges of a racist and segregated society, but in some measure failed to rally support at Lincoln to overcome the limitations of these practices.[8]

Laney used the confused and complex cultural milieu of his time to articulate his message about the value of a liberal arts education. He spoke of concern for the breakdown in the social fabric of society, especially the loss of trust, as evidenced by the savings and loans debacle, businessman Ivan Boesky and insider trading on Wall Street, and hostile takeovers in business. He spoke of former US Senator Gary Hart and the indiscretions in his personal relationships, and of television evangelist Jim Bakker and the fall of his PTL (Praise the Lord) empire due to his personal misuse of the organization's funds. He spoke of others who abused their positions of power and were brought down because of their abuse.[9]

For instance, in a baccalaureate address in 1987 titled "The Distinction Between a Lifestyle and a Life," Laney had this to say on the subject of Gary Hart: "The sadness of Gary Hart is that there was great ability, and I think a driving ambition, and in some sense, a real commitment to that life of public service. But the lure of a lifestyle unencumbered was too great for him."[10] From these examples of breakdown in public trust, Laney made a compelling case for what a liberal arts education could do to make society more moral and just.

Coupled with the breakdown in public trust was the rising sense of individual liberty and lack of civility practiced in society. Laney argued that an "ethos of disregard" pervaded all of society and needed to be corrected. In a speech in 1992 to a national gathering of United Methodists, he expressed this concern in this way:

> ...our dominant philosophy also has a down side—a kind of unrestrained individualism that ignores the social fabric. It tends to spawn an ethos of disregard. Individuals pursue their own interests, but those interests are sometimes terribly self-centered. The last few years have revealed what the excesses of *laissez-faire* individualism lead to when there is not a concomitant concern for larger responsibility.[11]

The combination of national loss of trust and the assertion of individual rights without regard for the common good was a significant theme in Laney's speeches and articles.

Major international shifts that took place in this era, creating freedoms for the oppressed, were also prevalent in Laney's communications. He referred with some frequency to the overthrow of apartheid in South Africa, the fall of the Berlin Wall and the end of the Cold War, and the fight for liberty in China at Tiananmen Square. He challenged his readers and listeners to contemplate what these changes meant to individual and national social practice and concern. In an address to the graduating seniors at Atlanta's Westminster Schools in 1992, Laney offered these reflections: "It is hard for me to comprehend that my entire adult life and probably those of your parents have been lived under the shadow of the Cold War, when national security dominated every agenda. Now suddenly all of that has changed, and we are struggling to come to terms with what the change means."[12] Among the real strengths of Laney's communications was his ability to offer comments that engaged crucial national and international changes, comments which encouraged the listener or reader to contemplate new ways of seeing and understanding the world.

Laney's observations, though, were not just limited to changes on the national and international scene. He spoke with great conviction about the challenges to the practices of higher education from critics such as William Bennett, Allan Bloom, and Ernest Boyer.[13] These writers sharply criticized higher education for its huge tuition increases, while reducing the amount of interaction between faculty and students and encouraging a politically correct curriculum. One of Laney's speeches explained the criticisms in this manner:

> In the past year, Secretary William Bennett has charged higher education with being rich and wanting to get richer, with charging too much tuition, and, most devastatingly, with not doing a good job. In this last charge, he was echoing Ernest Boyer's Carnegie report, which bemoaned the loss of the core curriculum and, along with it, the glories of our heritage and our sense of tradition and civility. Of course none of us in higher education likes to be criticized, so many of us pointed to increased costs and dismissed Secretary Bennett's position as simplistic.... I must acknowledge there is

> something very important in [his] remarks.... There is a
> growing uneasiness with higher education, an increasing
> resistance to it, a general disenchantment.[14]

Although Laney would not concede to the views of these "'cultural cheer-leaders,'"[15] he did believe that there was value in engaging them in dialogue, and attempting to dispel some of their concerns. He even identified common ground he shared with them, such as the commitment to free inquiry and the desire that the curriculum be socially useful.[16]

Laney was convinced that a return to the old way of teaching and using the Great Books, espoused also by Hutchins, as the cornerstone of the curriculum was not, finally, the solution. However, Laney gave the impression in his communications that even he struggled with what the proper solution should be, which was not an issue for Hutchins with his faculty. Hutchins' views and certainty on curricular issues resulted in the publication of *The Higher Learning in America*[17] in which he outlined a program of "'permanent studies' based on 'our intellectual inheritance' [which] would cultivate the 'intellectual virtues' useful for a life of contemplation or a life of action."[18] Sensing tension in 1989 at Emory between teaching and research and between the liberal arts and professional education, Laney made this comment to a faculty assembly: "The Arts and Sciences, the heart of American higher education, are overwhelmed if the role of teaching, of community, of the values of inherited wisdom—the arts—as well as science cannot properly be heard."[19] In this presentation, Laney expressed his concern that, at its most fundamental level, the university not be seen as "soulless," but as having a grounding and vision that were concerned with the common good of all.

Building on the societal changes and the challenges to higher education, Laney took care in offering through his speeches and writings an apologia for higher education. He did this by advancing what he believed to be the foundational mission of the university, namely to be a moral community of scholars. This understanding was expressed in his inaugural address in which he advocated that Emory should strive to be a "company of scholars," faculty and students working to keep alive questions of the common good.[20] This echoed a theme expressed by Hutchins five decades earlier that the curriculum should address "intellectually essential questions like those of existence and the purpose of human existence."[21]

Laney began his defense with a description of the origins of higher education, noting that education as a moral endeavor was at the heart of the higher education enterprise in the early years of this democracy. He often explained that those who founded Harvard and Yale were committed to these institutions promoting the social good through their educational agendas. While students were educated in a profession from which a wage could be earned, students were also steeped in the needs of society at large. Since the attainment of a higher education degree was so rare, graduates were compelled to be in service to their fellow human beings.[22] Laney wrote: "The intention of both charters [Harvard and Yale] was that in educating a younger generation, the schools would ensure that the commonwealth would be enhanced, the public good would be served, and individuals' increased learning would serve as a bulwark to public trust."[23] Given that the early role of the liberal arts was the advancement of a just, caring, and knowledgeable citizenry, Laney expressed concern that the dominant aspirations of today's student are power and material success, losing sight of the fact that service to others is really "greatness."[24]

Laney contended that the sense of concern for the commonweal was lost over the last century as "methodological secularism" became the dominant ethos, which was caused by the prominence of the scientific method and growth in pluralism. This change in ethos encouraged faculty to become more specialized in their disciplines and more loyal to their academic guilds.[25] Of necessity, faculty sought community with members of their guilds, most of whom were in other institutional settings, often to the neglect of faculty colleagues in different departments at their own institutions with offices only a few feet away. These tensions came to a head for higher education in the 1960s with the riots at Berkeley. Among other issues, students rioted against faculty who were unavailable as mentors, let alone as teachers. Faculty had become so preoccupied with their research interests that students felt closed out and alone.[26] Sadly, Laney could note in his 1987 sesquicentennial address to the Emory community that "Ironically, the very means by which our society and universities have achieved enormous distinction, constitute their Achilles heel. The rise of specialties, of subdisciplines within traditional disciplines, has largely removed the possibility of a shared discourse and common values."[27] For Laney, reaffirmation of the original idea of a liberal arts education as a moral endeavor pursuing the common good, while taking seriously the challenges of faculty life and practice, would, he hoped, restore a coherence and faith to higher education that it desperately needed.

Laney's View of Liberal Arts Education

Laney's speeches and articles allude to four elements which he believed were critical for a liberal arts education: a commitment to competence, a striving for the development of moral character, an offering of an inclusive community of learning, and an unyielding commitment to freedom of thought. This understanding was unique. As Stephen Nelson's study of the moral voice of college presidents shows, even though college presidents of this century have been concerned with the moral training of students, Laney's view of the totality of the liberal arts experience, especially the concern for the moral development of students, was, for his era at least, a new iteration.[28]

Laney contended that for education to be useful, students must be challenged to master the material they study. Developed and demonstrated competence in a field of choice is key to the educational process, a practice of higher education strongly urged by Eliot as early as 1869 in an attempt to provide more professionals for the growing society.[29] Laney held, however, that the emphasis on competence is a short-term commitment of the liberal arts institution because what the students learn now will soon be updated and expanded, and, in some cases, outdated, based on new research and scholarship.[30]

For Laney, the element of competence led to an ethos of professionalization in the academy. Laney noted that in this ethos students were given "…the tools of mastery and the credentials for entry into the world of work, but no longer [were they introduced] to the larger world of wisdom."[31] To overcome the careerist mentality of higher education, Laney advocated a longer view and a second element of education that required that the liberal arts be committed to the moral development of the student. On this essential, Laney, with his homiletical talent, honed by his years as a clergyman, waxed eloquent.

Laney averred that from the time of Aristotle, education has been concerned with the development of the character of the individual. Education should inform the whole life of the person by impressing upon the individual the need to care for and advance the public good. This was not, in Laney's eyes, a narrow indoctrination. Rather, it took seriously the true meaning of "liberal," which was to be broadminded and deeply convicted. It meant concern for one's fellow human beings and a willingness to serve those less fortunate. It meant acknowledging that within all persons "…there is a deeper hunger, a more enduring longing, an aspiration…a soul…that is not satisfied with merely the accumulation of the satisfaction of our desires."[32] For Laney, character development and the commitment of the individual to serve were inseparable from the competencies that should be cultivated in the student.

To achieve the moral development of the student, Laney held that the institution must foster additionally a moral community where differences in opinion and background are welcomed and civil discourse practiced. The moral community does not minimize participation; rather, it encourages the participation of all, by offering hospitality to the stranger and treating all participants as equals. It is where discourse occurs on some of the difficult topics of the day, with special emphasis on matters of faith and ultimate meaning. Laney described the community of the liberal arts institution as a "tableau of diverse peoples and many nations seated at a common meal, sharing bread and truth together."[33] He also used the analogy of the family, including his own, where with five children seated around the dinner table, there was the occasional kick under the table or insult uttered. The university, he believed, should be like a family where members could display their differences.[34]

In an opinion-editorial piece written for *The New York Times*, Laney advocated that the inclusive community must even tolerate bigots, for "…we cannot build up wisdom by tearing down people."[35] The inclusive community was not easy in Laney's view, but it was, for him, an essential element of a liberal arts education. When successful, the community fostered by the liberal arts frees students from the parochialism of fixed ideas, making students "unintimidated by pluralism."[36]

Implied in Laney's first three elements of competence, character, and community in the liberal arts institution was a critical fourth element, that of a commitment to freedom of thought. For the liberal arts community to build character through exposure to persons and opinions different from one's own, the time-honored commitment to free inquiry and free expression is essential. Laney was quick to note, however, that what is expressed requires thoughtful deliberation and careful articulation. Yet, the capacity of one's character to flourish and grow necessitates an openness to all forms of inquiry. On this point, Laney said, "Only in the freedom of the mind to question all things and to imagine all things can the human spirit seek its rightful home."[37] Through the freedom of thought provided by a liberal arts education, one should come to a sense of how one's energies, passions, and commitments should be lived out.

Laney argued that at its best the liberal arts institution, with its four essential characteristics, was, in the final analysis, the structural expression of love. He wrote: "Love is not generally what we are about in the university these days. It is not generally regarded as the university's cardinal virtue. But [it is appropriate] to think of the university as the structural expression of love, to think of the university's 'edification' in love...."[38] The direct result of this kind of educational experience is seen in students who show virtues needed to transform and strengthen society. Such virtues include honor, respect, courage, commitment to work, fidelity, goodwill, patience, discipline, restraint, and promise-keeping. Products of a liberal arts education know themselves. They have an inner and outer confidence that makes them leaders and models for others.[39] In a similar way, Hutchins advocated for morals in education, believing that this was the only means by which persons came to a greater understanding of themselves and their roles in the world. For Hutchins, morals and good habits were synonymous. He wrote, "By morals I mean good habits. Good habits are those which are good for the organism in question."[40]

Laney was at his most articulate when presenting his views on liberal arts education before church audiences and in religious settings. Given Emory's church relationship, Laney could with ease advocate that at its best a liberal arts education takes place in a church-related university. A church-related, liberal arts education for Laney was not a glorified Sunday School experience, however. Laney was clear that even though an institution might be affiliated with a denomination and committed to the purpose and ideals of that denomination, this association and commitment did not and could not diminish the academic rigor expected of faculty and students. If anything, the church-related nature of the institution required a commitment to the highest academic standards, in an environment that reflected a community of learning and service. In a 1988 speech before the Southeastern Jurisdictional Conference of the United Methodist Church, the body of the church with which Emory is affiliated, Laney said that Emory is "…a microcosm of American Society today, a microcosm which is encompassed and comprehended by people who care what goes on there and are determined that its direction and aspirations be consistent with Christian principles and teachings."[41] Laney described in this manner what moral development in the church-related university should achieve: "The link we find…between religious faith and good citizenship is the aspiration to create a better society—a society of strong democratic principles, respect for the individual, and material progress, all buttressed by a millennial faith in the imminent reign of God."[42] For Laney, it was inconceivable that church-related higher education could do anything other than focus on the moral development of the individual. Hutchins used similar arguments, although Chicago was thoroughly secular by the time of his arrival. Dzuback notes that Hutchins' commitment to the Great Books and to the centrality of philosophy in the school's curriculum was an attempt at a "contemporary translation of Oberlin's [Hutchins' undergraduate alma mater] nineteenth-century religious mission."[43]

In relation to Emory's church affiliation, Laney seemed to relish his role as baccalaureate speaker for Emory graduating seniors. Throughout his presidency he elected to speak on these occasions himself, as a way of replacing the now defunct tradition of the university president's teaching the senior capstone course on ethics.[44] The titles of Laney's addresses read as prescriptions for leading the good life, with titles such as "Choose Your Dreams Wisely," "The Strength of Vulnerability," "The True Nature of Authority," "The Possibilities of Limits," "Forging a Multicultural Family," "The Distinction Between a Lifestyle and a Life," "On Being an Honorable Person," "Mending the Social Fabric," and "Beyond the

Bottomline."[45] In 1993, in his final baccalaureate address titled "Power and Moral Authority," Laney had this to say to the graduates:

> Really what I am talking about is that maybe we have run our society too much on the basis of power and a kind of material definition of success, and that we have forgotten that greatness is really authority. Authority wins consent and endorsement. It does not impose itself on others simply because it can, but it exercises a kind of quiet influence that comes from representing things that all of us believe in and know are necessary. That is what we need in our society.[46]

Through these baccalaureate sermons Laney imparted, one last time, to the students his views on their moral obligations in the world.

Ingredients Critical for a Liberal Arts Education

To reaffirm the traditional focus of a liberal arts education, Laney identified three areas with which institutions must concern themselves. First, he contended that the liberal arts institution must provide sheltered space, which for him was a safe haven for free inquiry and deliberation and for the development of one's character. A shelter invites everyone in the community to value one another equally and to receive the offerings of others with an open mind and heart.[47] Laney wrote that the liberal arts institution in "its very educational mission thus serve[s] as a sheltered space, a ritual space, where questions of ultimate human and therefore spiritual significance c[an] be explored, regardless of any affiliations with religious bodies."[48] Thus, the shelter protects all and allows for the development of each human spirit. In a 1990 article in *Ethics in Higher Education,* Laney described the shelter as a "dwelling place for the human spirit—a habitation where faculty members, administrators, and students alike become habituated to a vision of the good society by inhabiting a good community of scholars."[49]

Along with the sheltered space of the liberal arts institution, Laney contended that a heightened commitment to students must be demonstrated by faculty. Faculty cannot be producers of research exclusively. The very calling of the professoriate requires that faculty see themselves as helpful role models and mentors for students. The traditional college-age years, Laney believed, are an impressionable time, as young people look about for persons in whom they can place their respect, trust, and confidence, persons who are seen by students as older, wiser, and stronger. The liberal arts institution provides an ideal environment for the one-to-one interaction between faculty and student that can result in life-transforming and life-giving relationships.[50] For Laney, the moral authority of the university resided in its calling to teach, because through teaching "...one invests in another life."[51] Among the many statements Laney made about the value of the mentor relationship between faculty and students, this one is typical: "This is why a liberal arts college is really the bellwether of tomorrow. It is the last place where, in fact, people invest themselves in a new generation. Members of the faculty get their greatest sense of reward and satisfaction from the light of a new idea in the mind of a student, or from the exciting chemistry of companionship."[52]

In a speech before the American Society of Clinical Pastoral Educators in 1977, Laney suggested that the care with which faculty treat their students has benefit for the faculty as well. He argued that since it is a fact of life that all persons want to be self-generative, faculty can satisfy this deep psychological yearning through the preparation and care given to those students who might follow in the faculty's footsteps. In this way, faculty replicate themselves and help advance their disciplines.[53]

The sheltered space of the college and the commitment of the faculty to mentor students, Laney argued, suggests a third and final element needed in today's institutions, and that is care and discrimination in the selection of faculty and students. To provide a community that is a microcosm of American society demands a commitment to inclusivity. Colleges are challenged to ensure that balance is achieved in the gender and racial make-up of the faculty and students, along with the intellectual capacities to handle the rigors of the academic environment. Equally important as inclusiveness, Laney argued, is selecting members of the community who support the mission of the institution. Choosing the right persons requires even greater powers of discernment than those needed for the academic abilities of the faculty or student because what is fundamentally sought is something much more nebulous, which is a personal quality in the individual that nurtures and supports community.[54]

Influences on Laney's View of Liberal Arts Education

Laney is a four-time graduate of Yale University.[55] His experience there, especially as an undergraduate and divinity student, impressed upon him the value of a liberal arts education. Based on his Yale experience, Laney believed that through the reading of history, English, religion, and sociology, students are introduced to "those ideas that shake us, and reformulate us, and help us to become properly free, so that we may reappropriate our own pasts with a new sense of power and passion."[56] Hutchins described the purpose of the liberal arts to "unsettle the minds" of students.[57]

For Laney, the leisure of his nearly seven-year, liberal arts odyssey (including his time in divinity school) opened his eyes to a world of thought and knowledge that his provincial, Southern upbringing had not afforded. The liberal arts courses themselves were not enough to transform his life; it took engaging, committed, and available teachers to inspire and motivate him. Martin Price in the undergraduate program,[58] Doug Cook in the co-curricular Wesley Fellowship,[59] and H. Richard Niebuhr in the divinity school[60] are mentioned from time to time in his speeches and writings on liberal arts education. In regard to his relationship to Niebuhr, Laney had this to say in one of his speeches:

> At Yale, I remember H. Richard Niebuhr, whose scholarship illumined a profound faith, and whose lectures often moved the students to a form of spiritual participation. We knew we were witnessing the articulation of the struggle of a soul.... The education we received would have been immeasurably impoverished without the influence of those kinds of lives.... We implicitly knew we were in the presence of people who shared enough of the common understanding of the Christian life that there was something to live up to. I don't recall having felt that as a peculiar burden, but as a source of deep pride.[61]

These relationships were truly life-changing for Laney, and they became a model for the mentor relationships he hoped Emory faculty would forge with their students.

Laney's understanding that liberal arts education can strengthen one by exposure to other cultures was heavily influenced by his tour of duty in Korea from 1946 until 1948 and his five years there as a missionary from 1959 until 1964. In one particularly moving address, Laney spoke about the difficulty of being in a foreign land when his child became deathly ill and he and his wife had no one to whom to turn, except God, in this moment of darkness and doubt,[62] and of the internal fortitude and confidence one gains from trying to make one's way in an environment so radically different from one's own. But he also knew the good that comes from relationships formed with people of different cultures, and how in learning about other cultures, one is also changed.[63]

Laney's conception of liberal arts education was not based exclusively on personal experience, but came from broad reading on the subject, influenced by his economics undergraduate major. Believing that liberal arts education was perhaps the best way to further the ends of a democratic society, Laney found the writings of non-American authors Walter Bagehot, Alexis de Tocqueville, and Adam Smith quite illuminating. In several communications, Laney referred to their awe of American democracy, especially the individual freedoms enjoyed and the sense of corporate commitment on the part of individuals to the commonweal. He described Bagehot, the author of an 1850 work titled *Physics and Politics*, as a "hard-headed economist and historian and realist" who tried to distill the secret of the success of the great societies of the world. That secret, according to Laney, was in the conception of moral character held before young people.[64]

As with Bagehot, Laney made numerous references to French philosopher Alexis de Tocqueville, author of the 1835 *Democracy in America*, about his observations of American democracy. Tocqueville noted that Americans had a spirit of vitality and commitment to each other and society that was lacking in Europe. Through this spirit, Americans were concerned as much for self as for others, and higher education institutions were viewed as key arenas for advancing the public good through the moral suasion of students.[65] Laney wrote that Tocqueville "showed how the association of townsfolk in clubs and churches and granges fostered a social cohesion that held communities together despite the centrifugal pull of individualism."[66]

Laney employed the writings of Adam Smith, the eighteenth-century economist, to great effectiveness in describing the need for a liberal arts education that is focused on the common good. Laney believed that

Smith was greatly misunderstood in that his best known work, *Wealth of Nations*, promoted the need for individual choice and individual pursuits to make for a successful and healthy capitalist society. This view, according to Laney, has led students of economic theory to believe that Smith advocated individual liberty at all costs over the success of social cohesion. Often overlooked, Laney held, was that Smith was a moral and social philosopher as well as an economist. In addition to *Wealth of Nations*, he wrote *The Theory of Moral Sentiments*, in which he advocated that individual liberty and choice can only succeed when there is concern for the greater good. Laney wrote that Smith saw that "capitalism has a stake in the moral climate of a society. Its leaders must embody those qualities and virtues which alone can ensure the well-being and total good of society. And its individual citizens must share a sense of labor and professionalism and public life that embraces...the notion of the common good."[67]

Laney rounded out his use of social/political thinkers in speeches and writing with Alasdair MacIntyre, who, like Bagehot, Tocqueville, and Smith, argued that a moral community is fostered by the development of virtue within individuals, a calling most appropriate for institutions of higher learning. Laney used MacIntyre's *Three Rival Versions of Moral Enquiry* and *After Virtue* to establish his claim about the need for a community of equality and sharing of values. MacIntyre believed that education is a moral activity "that has its own rewards and draws the [student] further and further along into its demands."[68] It is a practice or an activity that when done continually leads to greater skill and care in the carrying out of that duty, such as practice with a musical instrument or in preparation for athletic competition.[69]

Laney's exploration of the roles of a liberal arts education was not just limited to social/political thinkers. He also drew a great deal from literature, especially nineteenth-century writers George Eliot and Jane Austen. Eliot's writing captured for Laney the depth of human character and the capacity for humans to act for good under trying circumstances, despite human foibles. Laney described Eliot's understanding of "binocular vision" as the "capacity to see in depth, in perspective to see the world more broadly than one's self and one's own interests normally allow."[70] In particular, Laney seemed intrigued by Eliot's *Middlemarch*, where a young physician in his attempt to do good becomes confused about the difference between having a lifestyle and a life.[71] In baccalaureate address-es and speeches before large national audiences, Laney cited Eliot's work with regularity.[72]

The literary work of Jane Austen also captivated Laney, and he used references to her work as a way of demonstrating the need for a liberal education to develop students' moral sensibilities. In one presentation, Laney focused on Austen's *Mansfield Park*, in which the central character, Bertram, is seen as young, bright, and full of promise, but one who ulti-mately turns all of those who know him against him because he is so corrupt. Laney said that through characterizations such as Bertram, Austen "portrayed life with an exquisite moral sensibility [implying] that we need to address the accumulated wisdom in every culture and tradi-tion that says unbridled egoism is the surest road to hell."[73] For Laney, then, exposure to the writings of nineteenth-century authors such as Eliot and Austen, among many others, was one way a liberal arts educa-tion aided in the moral development of students.

Laney cited persons of great stature—contemporary moral heroes— who by their work, and less by their words, had an impact on him and who demonstrated what it meant to lead completely moral lives. This was true, for instance, of his encounters with Archbishop Desmund Tutu, who once on a visit to Laney's office asked to have prayer with Laney before their meeting began.[74] Laney also mentioned Jimmy Carter with great affection and admiration in a number of speeches. In speeches toward the end of his tenure as president, Laney discussed Carter's work with and commitment to the Atlanta Project, a grass roots effort to empower the poor and dispossessed to claim their rightful power and moral authority to make their lives and those of their neighbors better.[75] Laney also told of making the rounds one day with an Emory doctor, Ken Walker, at Grady Memorial Hospital. In a difficult visit with a patient who was dying of jaundice from years of alcohol abuse, Dr. Walker succeeded in getting the patient to talk about his condition and fear of the future by touching the patient on his feet and legs, where the jaundice was most pronounced. For Laney, Dr. Walker's action was a powerful metaphor that to advance the public good one has to touch before one can talk.[76]

Another source that guided Laney's outlook on liberal arts education and the moral life was the Bible. More than any other source, Laney cites biblical themes and individuals in baccalaureate sermons and academic addresses. In an address to the United Board of Christian Higher Education in Asia, a board that he at the time chaired, Laney had this to say about the value of the Bible: "The vision we need, of course, is a vision we get from the Bible—a vision that points us not only to the love of God and the love of neighbor, but also to an ethic that strives to keep the body politic healthy and whole. Biblical faith reminds us that opportunity, initiative, and enterprise must be balanced by fairness and justice."[77] For Laney, the Bible provided rules sufficient to exemplify how one should live in community.[78]

Biblical characters that received the most attention from Laney were King David[79] and Isaiah.[80] Laney found in the tragic figure of King David a remarkably honorable man, able to accept the fate he imposes on himself, and to give due honor and homage to those who earn and deserve it. Most important, though, was David's capacity to give honor to God, even in the most trying of circumstances. Laney was also drawn to the second chapter of Isaiah. The metaphor of the people climbing the mountain of the Lord suggested to Laney that in life all are equal because all are invited to climb the mountain. Moreover, God is seen as relational, willing to be in relationship with all who dare to climb the mountain. If God is willing to be so available to us, then why, Laney demurred, cannot liberal arts institutions provide hospitable, relational environments where all who enter the doors are considered equal and where God's spirit is invoked and believed to be operative?

Analysis of Laney's View of Liberal Arts Education

The files which contain Laney's unpublished speeches are filled with letters from appreciative listeners, many of whom Laney did not know.[81] If the letters are any indication, Laney's remarks about liberal arts education rang true for many. He seemed to advocate a position that many yearned for and hoped would become the prevailing paradigm for American higher education. If persons communicated their doubts about or criticisms of his positions, these letters were never placed in the files. Despite the absence of criticism in the archival files, there are several critiques of his speeches and writings that are worthy of consideration.

Perhaps the most obvious critique of the Laney speeches and articles is the idealism behind the argument he advanced. While the ideal of a liberal arts education was always communicated in a compelling and hopeful way, one wonders if Laney ever despaired about the realities of higher education and the extreme difficulty of fulfilling his vision. One might believe that had Emory adhered to Laney's vision the sense of community and the availability of faculty to students, especially as mentors, were never in question. To the contrary, Emory struggled with these issues during Laney's administration with limited success. Moreover, the tension between teaching and research in the faculty was never fully resolved in the awarding of tenure. Both Billy Frye and David Minter, provost and college dean respectively during Laney's presidency, acknowledge that because the university began attracting more renowned faculty during Laney's administration, research naturally carried the majority of the weight in tenure decisions.[82] Given this tension one wonders how Laney reconciled the emphasis on research with his own desire for faculty to be better teachers and mentors. In his speeches and addresses one hopes for more honest sharing of the difficulties in fulfilling the liberal arts vision, a charge similarly directed at Hutchins over his failure to acknowledge "educational research and social change" in the promotion of his curriculum reform effort at Chicago.[83]

A second criticism of Laney's view on the liberal arts is the surprise that over the nearly two decades of addressing this issue, the authorities he cited on the matter never seemed to change, and that the ones he selected—albeit well known and foundational—were dated, with the exception of the contemporary critics of higher education. One misses references to current writers, such as Mary Field Belenky[84], Carol Gilligan[85], and bell hooks.[86] Each one, from a uniquely feminist perspective, challenges the notions of what it means to be in community. It would be interesting to know, for instance, how Laney would describe the ideal collegiate community in light of Gilligan's claim that women's moral development is vastly different from that of men.[87] Would his view of community and the moral development encouraged in students be different from what he proposed? Thus, some attention to the writers outside the white male mainstream would have made his speeches even more compelling.

A third criticism of Laney's view of the liberal arts is his response to those he described as the "cultural cheerleaders" who challenged the practices of higher education in the 1980s and early 1990s. Laney went to some length to differentiate himself from the likes of Bennett and Bloom, but in many ways his critique of higher education did not differ from theirs. Like Bennett and Bloom, he agreed that the liberal arts had succumbed to the careerist mentality of the era, without regard for what could be done to advance the moral development of students. While Laney took exception to the Bennett proposal of the preservation of the

Western canon of the liberal arts curriculum, he did so because he was sufficiently broadened by his Asian experiences and studies in Christian ethics to know that the curriculum needed to include more than just Western writers. However, he was virtually silent on the matter of what the canon should include. In contrast, Hutchins, who wrote a book on the subject as noted earlier, advocated strongly for the Great Books program and the centrality of philosophy in the curriculum.

Laney no doubt knew that to advance a particular canon was doomed to failure because some group or individual would be disappointed by what he did not include, and he believed properly that such judgments were the province of the faculty exclusively. Yet, for all his passion for the moral development inherent in the liberal arts and for his opposition to Bennett and Bloom, it is strange that he did not advance an argument about what the curriculum should include. He was astute enough, however, to know that to provide an answer was a difficult challenge. In an address to Emory alumni in 1989 he observed: "Today we have to ask, *whose* common good is our goal? White males? Protestants? We must be sure that when we talk about education as privilege, we're not also talking about education as exclusive....The modern university is criss-crossed with complexities of science—it is not all in books anymore."[88] Yet, Laney could have helped the debates of the 1980s and early 1990s, and, perhaps, gained greater national visibility for himself and Emory, had he been bolder in advancing a curricular agenda. Instead, Laney stayed with the safer, albeit somewhat risky, issues of more meaningful mentor relationships between faculty and students and tenure practices and policies. Thus, Laney received the grateful attention of those who heard him or read him, but his proposals were not so out of the mainstream or visionary as to warrant the national attention gained by Bennett and Bloom.

It is said that any great preacher is usually preaching to her/himself, and in this statement there is a concluding observation about Laney. One gets the sense in reading Laney's speeches and articles that much of his commentary, while entirely appropriate for the audiences for which they were intended, was, in the end, directed at himself. In many ways, Laney exhibited a complex character of his own—a driven and ambitious man, with great dreams for Emory which he pursued with relentless vigor, and much success, but whose missionary and pastoral side caused him to question whether his ambitions for himself and Emory were being properly channeled. In an address to the Conference on Moral Values in Higher Education in 1987, Laney noted that major research universities are now huge conglomerates with a dark side:

> there's the competitive bidding for faculty, even the competitive *building* for research grants. We build new facilities, and we bid against each other for faculty stars, not just individuals, but whole teams of people. We build great departments like football teams. We're not adding to the sum total of knowledge or good; we're just moving the players around from here to there, and the price goes up accordingly.[89]

In less than three years from those comments, Emory made national news when it recruited nearly the entire French department, arguably the finest in the country, away from Johns Hopkins University.[90] As Laney noted in the speech above the ones who suffer most in this competition are the students, for whom higher education exists in the first place. Students become little more than a side show in this high-powered competition. Thus, one senses in Laney's speeches and articles an admonition to himself to balance more effectively the competing demands of increased university stature with the needs of the students enrolled in the institution.

Laney was not alone in either the complexity of his character or his desire to advance the interests of the institution over which he presided. Others before him, such as Eliot and Harper, dealt with similar challenges. For Eliot curriculum reform was a continual battle during his forty year tenure. He was not so much concerned about the moral climate of society as he was about helping students through a curriculum of electives to meet the practical needs of society, all the while attempting to keep pace with competitor institutions, such as Johns Hopkins. To stay competitive required a method that became a tradition, namely to raid the faculties of other institutions, such as MIT.[91] Likewise, Harper, in his zeal to build his empire at Chicago, conducted mass raids on college faculties around the country, hiring in his first year alone 120 new faculty members.[92] Yet, his troubled conscience about such acquisitions caused him to write to a friend, "It is not altogether a pleasant task to be lecturing in the University and trying to take away one of its professors at the same time."[93] Thus, Laney's ambitions for Emory and his actions, such as the French department acquisition from Johns Hopkins, were not unique; however, one still could have hoped for more honest sharing from him of his own internal struggles with these tensions and how he saw himself resolving them.

In the end, Laney's passionate commitment to liberal arts education, within the context of a church-related university, is one of the enduring legacies of his sixteen-year administration at Emory. The clarity with which he conveyed his convictions and the usually powerful metaphors he employed in his descriptions make his speeches, some of them nearly twenty years old now, still fresh and hopeful.

---

[1]Hugh Hawkins, *Between Harvard and America: The Educational Leadership of Charles W. Eliot* (New York: Oxford University Press, 1991) 291–92.

[2]Mary Ann Dzuback, *Robert M. Hutchins: Portrait of an Educator* (Chicago: University of Chicago Press, 1991) 2, 228.

[3]Wayne J. Urban, *Black Scholar: Horace Mann Bond 1904–1972* (Athens: University of Georgia Press, 1992) 94, 122, 137.

[4]See bibliography for a complete listing of all Laney speeches and articles.

[5]Frederick Rudolph, *The American College and University: A History* (New York: Alfred A. Knopf, Inc., 1983) 336.

[6]Dzuback, *Robert M. Hutchins*, 83.

[7]Dzuback, *Robert M. Hutchins*, 84.

[8]Urban, *Black Scholar*, 134–36.

[9]From his speeches and articles, a sampling that touches these matters includes: James T. Laney, "Birthright and Blessing," May 1992, *The Education of the Heart: Selected Speeches of James T. Laney*, (Atlanta: Emory University, 1994) 97–105; hereafter, all speeches from this publication will be designated by *Heart*; James T. Laney, "The Distinction Between a Lifestyle and a Life," May 1987, *Heart*, 107–12; James T. Laney, "The Possibilities of Limits," May 1989, *Heart*, 113–22; James T. Laney, "A New Way of Seeing for a New Global Society," May 1990, *Heart*, 121–28; James T. Laney, *Our Mission in Higher Education: Vision and Reality*, Presidential Papers, vol. 8, no. 3 (Nashville: Division of Higher Education, Board of Higher Education and Ministry, The United Methodist Church, September 1992) 1–4; James T. Laney, "Choose Your Dreams Wisely," May 1981, *Emory Magazine* (Fall 1981): 12–13; James T. Laney, "Mending the Social Fabric: A Baccalaureate Address," *Emory Magazine* (September 1992): 13–14; James T. Laney, "Power and Moral Authority: A Baccalaureate Address," *Emory Magazine* (May 1993): 13–14.

[10]Laney, "The Distinction Between a Lifestyle and a Life," 109.

[11]Laney, *Our Mission in Higher Education: Vision and Reality*, 2.

[12]James T. Laney, "Graduation Address: Westminster Schools," 16 May 1992, Laney Papers, box 25-1, pocket 7, RWWL, 1. For additional references see James T. Laney, "Through Thick and Thin: Two Ways of Talking about the Academy and Moral Responsibility," in *Ethics in Higher Education*, ed. William W. May (New York: American Council on Education, 1990) 49–66; James T. Laney, "Presidential Leadership for Shared Values in Pluralist Communities: The Issue and the Challenge," January 1991, *Heart*, 21–30; Laney, *Our Mission in Higher Education: Vision and Reality*, 2.

[13]William J. Bennett, *The War over Culture in Education* (Washington, DC: Heritage Foundation, 1991); William J. Bennett, *The De-Valuing of America: The Fight for Our Culture and Our Children* (New York: Summitt Books, 1992); Allan Bloom, *The Closing of the American Mind: How Higher Education Has Failed Democracy and Impoverished the Souls of Today's Students* (New York: Simon and Schuster, 1987); Ernest L. Boyer, *College: The Undergraduate Experience in America*

(New York: HarperCollins Publishers, 1987); Ernest L. Boyer, *Scholarship Reconsidered: Priorities of the Professoriate* (Princeton: Carnegie Foundation for the Advancement of Teaching, 1990).

[14]James T. Laney, "Conference on Moral Values in Higher Education," 12–14 February 1987, Laney Papers, box 25-1, pocket 3, RWWL, 1.

[15]Laney, "Presidential Leadership for Shared Values," 26.

[16]Laney, "Presidential Leadership for Shared Values," 26.

[17]Robert Maynard Hutchins, *The Higher Learning in America* (New Brunswick NJ: Transaction Publishers, 1995). Originally published by Yale University Press in 1936.

[18]Dzuback, *Robert M. Hutchins*, 125.

[19]James T. Laney, "Remarks to General Faculty Assembly," September 1989, Laney Papers, box 25-1, pocket 5, RWWL, 7.

[20]James T. Laney, "Remarks in Response to Installation," March 1978, Laney Papers, box 25-2, folder "Correspondence, Speeches, and Clippings," RWWL.

[21]Dzuback, *Robert M. Hutchins*, 96.

[22]James T. Laney, "Liberal Arts Colleges and the Future of Higher Education," April 1989, *Heart*, 73; James T. Laney, "Hope and Purpose for this Day," *Emory Magazine* (Fall 1992): 2; James T. Laney, "Education and the Common Good," 30 March 1989, Laney Papers, box 25-1, pocket 4, RWWL; Laney, "Through Thick and Thin," 52–53.

[23]Laney, "Through Thick and Thin," 52.

[24]Laney, "Mending the Social Fabric," 13.

[25]James T. Laney, "'The Purpose of the College': Reaffirming the Wofford/Emory Ideal for the 21st Century," 19 February 1991, Laney Papers, box 2, pocket 6, RWWL.

[26]James T. Laney, "The Education of the Heart," October 1984, *Heart*, 61.

[27]James T. Laney, "A Sense of Larger Purpose: A Sesquicentennial Convocation Address," *Emory Magazine* (March 1987): 11.

[28]Stephen James Nelson, "A Study of the Moral Voice of the College President" (Ph.D. diss.: University of Connecticut, 1996) 48–58.

[29]Hawkins, *Between Harvard and America*, 58–59.

[30]James T. Laney, "Reevaluating Liberal Education," July 1988, *Heart*, 68.

[31]Laney, "Conference on Moral Values in Higher Education,"Laney Papers, 4.

[32]Laney, "The Distinction Between a Lifestyle and a Life," 109. For additional references on this topic see Laney, "Education of the Heart," 62; James T. Laney, "The Moral Authority of the President," April 1983, *Heart*, 3; James T. Laney, "A Future for Research," *Emory Magazine* (Fall 1977): 11; James T. Laney, "Laney Contribution to the Randolph-Macon Sequicentennial [sic] Celebration Volume,"

January 1980, Laney Papers, box 25-1, pocket 1, RWWL, 1; James T. Laney, "Annual Meeting of Board of Visitors: James T. Laney Remarks," 23 April 1986, Laney Papers, box 25-1, pocket 3, RWWL, 11; Laney, "Education and the Common Good," 9; James T. Laney, "Annual Board of Visitors Meeting: James T. Laney Remarks," 12 May 1993, Laney Papers, box 25-1, pocket 7, RWWL, 6; Laney, "Through Thick and Thin," 61.

[33]James T. Laney, *The Moral Purpose of the University* (Indianapolis: The Lilly Endowment, 1995) 20. Other speeches pertaining to this topic include "A New Way of Seeing for a New Global Society"; "The Moral Authority of the President," 6; "'The Purpose of the College,'" 8; James T. Laney, "Address to Parents," 27 August 1988, Laney Papers, box 25-1, pocket 4, RWWL, 3; James T. Laney, "Success in the Service of an Important Cause," August 1988, *Heart*, 18.

[34]"New Way of Seeing," 125–26.

[35]James T. Laney, "Why Tolerate Campus Bigots?," *The New York Times*, 6 April 1990, A35.

[36]Laney, "Reevaluating Liberal Education," 76.

[37]Laney, *The Moral Purpose of the University*, 6. See also James T. Laney, *Free Speech and the Freedom to Speak*, Presidential Papers, vol. 6, no. 1 (Nashville: Division of Higher Education and Ministry, Board of Higher Education and Ministry, The United Methodist Church, April 1990) 3.

[38]Laney, *Free Speech and the Freedom to Speak*, 20.

[39]A number of Laney's speeches make reference to the characteristics found in the products of a liberal arts education. See especially "Address to Parents"; *The Moral Purpose of the University*, 20; "The Education of the Heart," 60; James T. Laney, "Oxford College Graduation," 11 June 1977, Laney Papers, box 25-1, pocket 1, RWWL; James T. Laney, "Baccalaureate Address, Emory University," 10 June 1979, Laney Papers, box 25-1, pocket 1, RWWL.

[40]Robert Maynard Hutchins, *Freedom, Education and the Fund: Essays and Addresses, 1946–1956* (New York: Meridan Books, 1956) 81–82.

[41]James T. Laney, "Speech to the Southeastern Jurisdictional Assembly of the United Methodist Church," 15 July 1988, Laney Papers, box 25-1, pocket 4, RWWL.

[42]Laney, "'The Purpose of the College.'" Other references include "Address to Parents of Freshman Class '92"; James T. Laney, "Address to Rotary Club of Atlanta," 3 October 1977, Laney Papers, box 25-1, pocket 1, RWWL; James T. Laney, "Address to Northside Kiwanis Club," 23 September 1977, Laney Papers, box 25-1, pocket 1, RWWL; "The Moral Authority of the President."

[43]Dzuback, *Robert M. Hutchins*, 104.

[44]Laney, "Choose Your Dreams Wisely," 12. Laney continued a practice adopted by Harper some ninety years before him. Laney, no doubt, would have concurred

with an observation made by Harper after speaking with students about religion and the higher life that, "'I have in this way discharged in a measure of responsibility which has weighed upon me more heavily than any other connected with the office which I have been called to administer'" (Richard Storr, *Harper's University: The Beginning* [Chicago: University of Chicago Press, 1966] 184).

[45]See bibliography for complete information on these speeches.

[46]Laney, "Power and Moral Authority," 13.

[47]Laney, "'The Purpose of the College,'" 12.

[48]Laney, *The Moral Purpose of the University*, 3.

[49]Laney, "Through Thick and Thin," 59.

[50]Laney, "Liberal Arts Colleges and the Future of Higher Education," 78; "'The Purpose of the College,'" 11; "Rotary," 3; "Kiwanis," 4; "The Moral Authority of the President," 8.

[51]Laney, "Education and the Common Good," 9.

[52]Laney, "Reevaluating Liberal Education," 79–80.

[53]Laney, "Education as Identification," 9 November 1977, Laney Papers, box 25-1, pocket 1, RWWL, 3.

[54]Laney, "Randolph Macon Sequicentennial [sic] Publication."

[55]In addition to a B.A., B.D. and Ph.D., Laney was also awarded the L.H.D. in 1993.

[56]Laney, "Liberal Arts Colleges and the Future of Higher Education," 77.

[57]Dzuback, *Robert M. Hutchins*, 92.

[58]Laney, "Liberal Arts Colleges and the Future of Higher Education," 80; "Remarks to Faculty Assembly," 9.

[59]Laney, "Remarks to Faculty Assembly," 9. Cook is not mentioned by name, but is referred to as someone in attendance at the assembly meeting that Laney would not embarrass by identifying him.

[60]Laney, "The Moral Authority of the President," 8.

[61]James T. Laney, "The Purpose of a University Divinity School," April 1983, *Heart*, 93.

[62]James T. Laney, "Baccalaureate Sermon," May 1984, Laney Papers, box 34C, folder 1.10, RWWL, 5–6.

[63]Laney, "A New Way of Seeing for a New Global Society," 124.

[64]Laney, "Kiwanis," 4; "Rotary," 6; James T. Laney, "Moral Authority in the Professions," March 1986, *Heart*, 39; James T. Laney, "Address Given to the General Board of Global Ministries," 12 March 1984, Laney Papers, box 25-1, pocket 2, RWWL, 1.

[65]James T. Laney, "Sesquicentennial Convocation Address," *Emory Magazine* (12 January, 1987): 6; and "'The Purpose of the College,'" 7. James. T. Laney, "The

Law: A Moral Aristocracy," March 1993, *Heart*, 52; *Mitre and Mortar Board: What Happens When the Ancient Office of Bishop Meets the Modern American College Board of Trustees*, Occasional Papers, no. 78 (Nashville: United Methodist Board of Higher Education and Ministry, 15 June 1989) 2; "Mending the Social Fabric," 12; "Graduation Address: Westminster Schools," 3–4.

[66]Laney, "Through Thick and Thin," 58–59.

[67]James T. Laney, "The Other Adam Smith," *Economic Review* (October 1981): 29. See also Laney, "Moral Authority in the Professions," 39; "The Law: A Moral Aristocracy," 51; "Our Mission in Higher Education: Vision and Reality," 2; "Mending the Social Fabric," 12; James T. Laney, "Report to Board of Visitors," 13 May 1992, Laney Papers, box 25-1, pocket 7, RWWL, 5–6; "Through Thick and Thin," 56–57.

[68]Laney, *The Moral Purpose of the University*, 15. See also Laney, "'The Purpose of the College,'" 6.

[69]Laney, "Through Thick and Thin," 59–60.

[70]Laney, *The Moral Purpose of the University*, 20.

[71]Laney, "The Distinction Between a Lifestyle and a Life," 109.

[72]Other speeches with references to Eliot include, "Baccalaureate Address, 1979," 2; "Liberal Arts Colleges and the Future of Higher Education," 76; "Address to Freshmen," 2; and James T. Laney, "Religion and the Open University: A Report from the Front," no date, Laney Papers, box 25-1, pocket 6, RWWL, 15.

[73]Laney, "Education and the Common Good," 7. Also, Laney, "Birthright and Blessing," 99.

[74]Laney, "Power and Moral Authority: A Baccalaureate Address," 13.

[75]Laney, "Power and Moral Authority: A Baccalaureate Address," 13; and "Mending the Social Fabric: A Baccalaureate Address," 13.

[76]"Liberal Arts Colleges and the Future of Higher Education," 80; James T. Laney, "How is Jesus the Lord of History?," Joe Hale, ed., *Proceedings of the Sixteenth World Methodist Conference* (Lake Junaluska NC: The World Methodist Council, 1992) 196–97.

[77]James T. Laney, "Message From the Chair to the United Board of Christian Higher Education in Asia," July 1992, Laney Papers, box 21-2, folder UBCHEA, RWWL, 2.

[78]Laney, "'The Purpose of the College,'" 10.

[79]Laney, "Baccalaureate Sermon," May 1984, 2; James T. Laney, "The Tree that Gives Good Fruit: A Baccalaureate Address," *Emory Magazine* (August 1989): 22; Laney, "Baccalaureate Address, June 1979," 4; James T. Laney, "The True Nature of Authority: A Baccalaureate Address," *Emory Magazine* (July 1985): 22.

[80]James T. Laney, "An Unlikely Strength: A Baccalaureate Sermon," May 1983, Laney Papers, box 34C, folder 1.9, RWWL, 4; Laney, "The Tree That Gives Good Fruit: A Baccalaureate Address," 21; James T. Laney, "Chairman's Message to the Annual Meeting of the United Board for Christian Higher Education in Asia," June 1990, Laney Papers, box 21-2, folder UBCHEA, RWWL, 3.

[81]See especially Laney Papers, boxes 25-1 and 25-2, RWWL.

[82]Billy E. Frye, interview by author, tape recording, Emory University, Atlanta, 23 June 1998; David Minter, telephone conversation with author, LaGrange GA, 7 July 1998. See also Howard R. Bowen and Jack H. Schuster, *American Professors: A National Resource Imperiled* (New York: Oxford University Press, 1986) 19.

[83]Dzuback, *Robert M. Hutchins*, 139.

[84]Mary Field Belenky, *Women's Ways of Knowing: The Development of Self, Voice, and Mind* (New York: Basic Books, 1986).

[85]Carol Gilligan, *In a Different Voice: Psychological Theory and Women's Development* (Cambridge MA: Harvard University Press, 1982).

[86]bell hooks, *Talking Back: Thinking Feminist, Thinking Black* (Boston: South End Press, 1989).

[87]Gilligan, *In a Different Voice*, 65ff.

[88]Laney, "Education and the Common Good," 3.

[89]Laney, "Conference on Moral Values in Higher Education," 8.

[90]Don Wycliff, "Emory Raises Its Status," *The New York Times*, 23 August 1990, A18. The article notes that "raiding faculties of top universities is a route to the top."

[91]Hawkins, *Between Harvard and America*, 62–65.

[92]Rudolph, *The American College and University*, 350–51; Storr, *Harper's University*, 68–75.

[93]Laurence Veysey, *The Emergence of the American University* (Chicago: University of Chicago Press, 1965) 369.

CHAPTER THREE

THE BIG GIFT

A university presidency in the latter twentieth and early twenty-first centuries requires significant attention to fund-raising. Along with speech-making activities through which the president imparts his/her vision for the institution, there is likely no greater task to which the president must be committed than that of raising funds for the institution.[1] While fund-raising is perhaps the primary task of the university president in the late twentieth century, it is a responsibility with which most university presidents in all eras have contended. Of all college presidents, Eliot, perhaps, had it easiest. Financing for Harvard was a concern at times, but it is notable that tuition increased very little during Eliot's forty year tenure—remaining at approximately $150 per year—and that most gifts to Harvard came without direct solicitation.[2] Harper's relationship with Rockefeller was crucial in securing the funding necessary to make Chicago financially viable. Both prior to and soon after the founding of Chicago, Harper spent considerable time with Rockefeller attempting to discern Rockefeller's interests while matching those interests to Harper's grandiose plan of what a new national university should be.[3] The relationship Hutchins and Bond enjoyed with funders, especially with the Rockefeller Foundation for Hutchins at Chicago and the Rosenwald Fund for Bond at Fort Valley and Lincoln, proved at times to be relationships of saving grace and utter disappointment. In 1936, for instance, Hutchins was pleased to secure a $3 million contribution from the Rockefeller Foundation, but, by 1939, he sensed that the Rockefeller Foundation could no longer be counted on to help Chicago with growing disparities in its budget.[4] Bond and Fort Valley were encouraged by investments of the Rosenwald Fund and others that resulted in a doubling of Fort Valley's income during Bond's six year tenure. Yet, a souring of Bond's relationship with Embree of the Rosenwald Fund, which began while Bond was at Fort Valley, led to no financial support from the Rosenwald Fund while Bond was at Lincoln.[5] Laney's tenure as president of Emory cannot be fully understood without a thorough review of the most significant event of his administration, which was the gift in 1979 of $105 million from Coca-Cola magnate brothers, Robert and George Woodruff, a gift that at the time was the largest ever in US philanthropy.

That Robert W. Woodruff should have made such a magnanimous gift to Emory in 1979 is, at one level, surprising, given the nature of the relationship Woodruff had with Emory during his lifetime. Two events in the Woodruff-Emory relationship would have led the casual observer to conclude that such generosity from one of America's wealthiest corporate leaders could never occur. The first event took place in late fall 1908, when the young Woodruff was completing his first quarter at Emory College. Emory at the time was still a college—not to achieve university status until 1915—located in Oxford, some thirty miles east of Atlanta. Then, as now, the social life of students in Oxford, especially on the weekends, took them to Atlanta to enjoy the distractions of this urban environment. Woodruff, who had joined a fraternity, seemed more inclined to the social life of college that could be experienced in Atlanta and less to the academic opportunities it afforded.

Woodruff's father was Ernest Woodruff, who had started a bank in Atlanta in 1891, which later became Trust Company Bank and then SunTrust Bank. Concerned about his son's poor academic success at Emory, and, perhaps, not wanting to believe that his son was not up to the academic challenges, but, if true, not wanting needlessly to pay his tuition, Ernest Woodruff wrote to then-President James E. Dickey, the following plea: "It is very unfortunate that Robert's eyes are troubling him to such an extent that it appears useless to keep him at college. If there is no improvement...I would thank you for letting him come home." Convinced that Robert's problem was motivational and not physical, Dickey wrote father Woodruff this terse response: "I do not think it advisable for him to return to college this term as he has not done satisfactory work. He has never learned to apply himself which, together with very frequent absences, makes it impossible for him to succeed as a student."[6] The opinion of the president, so directly stated, prevailed, and Robert dropped out of Emory in early 1909, never to return as a student to Emory or to any other institution of higher learning. That Robert Woodruff did not hold a grudge against Emory, both for his failure to succeed academically and for the embarrassment President Dickey caused him with his father, is noteworthy.

Laney believes that in looking back on his life, Woodruff came to appreciate the academic integrity that Emory and President Dickey tried to maintain, namely that a young adult of some means and from an influential family would not be permitted to ride roughshod over Emory's expectations of academic achievement and excellence from its students. Instead of creating resentment within Woodruff toward Emory, the dismissal created a sense of awe for Emory and its mission.[7]

As Laney came to know Woodruff, Laney discovered that Woodruff revered him because he was the president. At parties or events hosted by Woodruff with Laney in attendance, Laney would always be seated next to Woodruff, as a sign of his special favor with Woodruff, in part because of the relationship Laney had forged with Woodruff, but in part because Laney held the office of president.[8] In fact, it was not until 1979 that Woodruff would consider himself worthy enough—after strong coaxing by Laney—to accept an honorary doctorate from Emory, one that Emory had attempted to bestow on him many times since 1942 for his beneficence to Emory and Atlanta.[9]

Woodruff's appreciation, if not affection, for Emory was deepened early on when he ascended in 1923, at the young age of thirty-three, to the chief executive officer's position of Coca-Cola Company, a company his father had purchased only four years earlier from the Candler family. The Candler family had very close ties to Emory. Bishop Warren Candler—former president of Emory College and the chairman of the committee of the Methodist Episcopal Church, South, that chose Atlanta over Birmingham as the site for the denomination to found a new institution of higher learning—was brother to Asa Griggs Candler, who started Coca-Cola and who gave the initial endowment gift of $1 million to establish the new university. The efforts of these brothers had made Emory a central player in the development of Atlanta as an urban center. Thus, Woodruff knew of the importance of Emory, not only to higher education, but to the fortunes of Atlanta. If he harbored any animosities toward Emory for its dismissal of him as a student, he overcame them quickly, and saw to it that Coca-Cola and the Candler family's support of the university continued.[10]

In 1935, Woodruff accepted appointment to Emory's board of trustees. By this time a tripartite relationship—perhaps unparalleled anywhere else in the country—developed between corporation, bank, and university. While Woodruff continued to run Coca-Cola and build it into one of the best known companies in America, if not the world, Woodruff's father's stewardship of Trust Company had been successful as well. In addition to providing the banking services for Coca-Cola, Trust Company also oversaw the financial affairs of Emory. Emory owned Coca-Cola stock, much of it given by the Candler family earlier and never sold, and, as a result, Emory was a significant shareholder of the company.[11] Thus, Woodruff's acceptance of the offer to serve on the board was motivated both by civic obligation and the desire to see that two companies important to his family—Coca-Cola and Trust Company—were successful.

Two years after Woodruff's appointment to the board his mother developed cancer, an illness that years before had taken her father's life. As cancer carried with it a negative social stigma in those years, and wanting to preserve his mother's life, Robert, along with his younger brother, George, gave the medical school at Emory $50,000 to establish a tumor clinic to treat cancer.[12]

This initial gift in 1937 began what became a close personal and financial investment in the fortunes of Emory's medical program. Woodruff became close friends with each of the vice presidents who oversaw health affairs at Emory, with each one becoming his personal physician during his tenure. By 1944, wanting the medical program to flourish, Woodruff and his brother, through the Woodruff Foundation, established at the deaths of their parents, began a major financial investment in the medical program of nearly $400,000 per year. By 1953, they had committed $5 million to establish a medical center that would include medicine, dentistry, and nursing. By 1979, the date of their landmark gift to Emory, Robert and George Woodruff had contributed in excess of $110 million to Emory, mostly for medical purposes.[13]

In 1957, a second event occurred that caused some members of the board of trustees to worry that Woodruff might withdraw his support from the university, despite his assurances to the contrary: he declined re-election to the board of trustees. Woodruff believed it prudent for Emory that he not serve again, and that a younger person be elected in his place. He conveyed these sentiments in a letter to Bishop Arthur J. Moore, the vice chairman of the board of trustees, offering this prescient conclusion: "You know, of course, of my general satisfaction with the organization of the Board and the operation of the University and I assure you that I will always be of any possible service. It is unnecessary to add, I'm confident, that Emory and its welfare will continue to be one of my principal interests in life."[14]

There were two reasons for concern. First, Woodruff expressed "general satisfaction" with the University, and not full support. This led to a second concern, namely that six months prior Emory had elected a new president—Sidney Walter Martin, dean of the college at the University of Georgia and strong Methodist layman. Support for Martin's appointment was not universal. Faculty who had had occasion to visit with Martin during the interview process had their doubts about him. Two weeks prior to his election on 13 April 1957, eleven key department chairs at Emory wrote to Charles Howard Candler, chairman of the board of trustees, the following: "It is our judgment that he [Martin] does not incorporate personally or professionally that combination of qualities so essential for vigorous and effective guidance of Emory's future destiny."[15] Woodruff, too, had had occasion to interview Martin prior to his election. While there is no recorded evidence that Woodruff opposed Martin's election, there was fear that Woodruff was expressing his dissatisfaction by not seeking reelection.[16] So as to leave no doubt with Woodruff about his continuing importance to Emory, Bishop Moore sent a letter to Woodruff two days later, which included: "Of course, we would have liked very much to have had you serve as a Trustee of Emory University, but knowing your devotion to Emory and the heavy responsibilities you carry, I accept your verdict in the matter. You greatly comfort me and all the rest of us by your assurance that Emory will be one of your principal interests."[17] As the historical record now shows, the concern about Woodruff's potentially negative attitude toward Emory was unfounded, but in 1957 there was concern, and doubt, that a gift of major proportions could ever come Emory's way.

Until 1979, the Woodruff philanthropy to Emory was focused almost exclusively on the medical program. The relationship Woodruff continued to have to the university was mostly through its vice presidents for health affairs. Presidents Martin and Atwood visited occasionally with

Woodruff, but neither could be described as having a close relationship with him.

Laney's relationship to Woodruff was warmer and more cordial than those his predecessors enjoyed, principally because Laney was shrewd, albeit sincere, in developing it. Chapter 1 details the initial meeting in 1975 that Laney, as dean of Candler, had with Woodruff at a social gathering. Out of that meeting grew an invitation for Laney to visit in his home during the early evening hours, an invitation that Laney accepted. By the time of the search for Atwood's successor, Woodruff was convinced that Laney was the person for the job, and expressed this view in a letter to Henry Bowden, chairman of the board and of the search committee.[18]

Once Laney was the occupant in the president's office, he took greater liberties to ingratiate himself and Emory to Woodruff. Whereas the cadre of Woodruff associates and colleagues would visit in Woodruff's home from 5:00 P.M. until 7:00 P.M. during the week, Laney would go earlier, around 4:00 P.M. or 4:30 P.M. to have Woodruff's undivided attention.[19] Their relationship became so close that Woodruff invited Laney to call him by his first name. Yet, given that Woodruff could not fathom referring to Laney as "Jim" (instead of "Dr. Laney"), Laney could not fathom referring to Woodruff as anything other than "Mr. Woodruff."[20] Still, their relationship became deeply personal, and Laney became for Woodruff a surrogate spiritual mentor. In addition to personal visits, Laney also wrote and phoned Woodruff. This handwritten letter from Laney to Woodruff in 1977 dated and sent to arrive likely on Christmas Eve—less than six months after Laney had been in office—is typical of his communications with Woodruff:

Dear Mr. Woodruff:

At Christmas one's thoughts turn naturally to gifts and gratitude.

Since assuming the presidency I have been privileged to learn even more about the extraordinary magnitude of your generosity to Emory. I am awed and amazed. Surely there is no parallel in all of higher education, either in this country or abroad.

The only appropriate response in appreciation is to pledge to you that Emory will continue to grow in stature, and that your investments here will appreciate in every conceivable way.

I can imagine how proud you must be of what you have accomplished here. I am proud to be associated with you in carrying on that remarkable legacy.

Merry Christmas![21]

These contacts between Laney and Woodruff were important because they developed an intimacy in their relationship that permitted them to deal directly with each other on matters that concerned the university rather than having others interpret Laney to Woodruff or Woodruff to Laney.

The true sign of one's favored status with Woodruff was to be among the approximately eight people he invited to join him for his birthday celebrations on 6 December of each year at Ichauway Plantation. Laney was not invited to the birthday celebration in 1977, Laney's first year in office. Yet, this did not deter him from being in Woodruff's presence on that day. Laney made arrangements through Woodruff's personal secretary to have a thirty-minute meeting with Woodruff on 6 December 1977. The purpose of the visit was to share with Woodruff an audiotape of a broadcast Alistar Cooke had done on his weekly BBC radio broadcast. Earlier in the fall, Cooke had consented to be the annual Bobby Jones Lecturer at the Law School. Cooke was apparently so taken by the Southern hospitality he experienced and the potential he saw in Emory that his entire broadcast that week was devoted to his Emory visit. In his show, Cooke explained to the audience that of the sixty or seventy college campuses he had visited none compared to the beauty of the Emory campus. He said, "I would vote with no other competitor in sight for the campus of Emory University in Atlanta." He added that, "...visiting Emory was like walking out of ancient Britain into the Garden of Eden."[22] Laney was thrilled with the piece, especially the international exposure it gave Emory.

Laney played the recording for Woodruff in the 1977 visit. While Laney doubts Woodruff could understand much of the tape, because of hearing difficulty, he is certain that Woodruff got the message that Emory had the potential to become an international university.[23] In addition to the message of Emory's promise that he wanted Woodruff to hear, Laney also got something else during this visit: an invitation to every subsequent birthday celebration at Ichauway. Laney was now among Woodruff's favored friends and associates.

At the 1978 birthday celebration, Woodruff called on Laney to give the blessing for the dinner, which he did extemporaneously. Woodruff liked it so much that he asked Laney for a copy, which Laney later wrote and sent to Woodruff. It read:

> We thank thee, Lord for this glorious day, and for the very special event we celebrate here, the 89th birthday of Mr. Woodruff. We acknowledge before Thee his towering presence through the years and across the land: his unexcelled generosity, his commanding vision, his unswerving loyalty; And praise Thee for the countless numbers who have been blessed through him, inspired

by his courage, strengthened by his determination, enabled by support. Bless him, O Lord, in the coming years, and grant him deep satisfaction and fulfillment, and a full measure of thy peace and serenity. Now give us festive hearts and true affection as we celebrate together this special day about this table, and keep care of us within the circle of your tender care. Through Christ our Lord. Amen.[24]

Laney's masterful weaving of words on the occasion of this birthday so touched Woodruff that he requested that this prayer be read at each subsequent birthday celebration, which it was until his death.[25]

At the time of Laney's inauguration in April 1978, Laney wanted the event to be memorable, and he wanted Emory's most generous benefactor to be present, as a sign of his support of the new administration. Woodruff attended, and in what seemed an impromptu act prior to his installation speech, Laney recognized Woodruff, came from the podium to the front row where Woodruff was seated and shook his hand. The audience was moved by the gesture, and in grateful response Woodruff received a standing ovation. Actually, Laney had been working behind the scenes for quite some time to pull off the recognition. Several memoranda in Woodruff's files testify to this fact, but one sent to Woodruff just two days prior to the event by Boisfeuillet Jones, the chairman of the Woodruff Fund, shows just how elaborate the plan was. Jones wrote in part:

> During his remarks and without previous notice, Dr. Laney will make some appropriate reference to you, acknowledge your presence, and come from the platform to where you are sitting to identify you to the audience. You may wish to stand and shake his hand, or remain

seated and shake his hand. It would not be appropriate for you to say anything, but you may wish quietly to thank and congratulate Dr. Laney.[26]

Laney's recognition of Woodruff was a stroke of genius in that Woodruff seldom attended public events, and in that Woodruff preferred anonymity for all he did. On this occasion, however, the presence of Woodruff and Laney's recognition of him signaled just how strong the bond between the two of them had become.[27]

After the inauguration, Laney's visits with Woodruff continued but they were not limited to issues of a personal and spiritual nature. Laney took care to share his vision for Emory's future and the financial needs it faced. Soon after becoming president, Laney alerted the trustees that the needs of Emory were so great that a capital funds drive would be needed to raise in excess of $100 million. The trustees eventually gave their blessing. An internal committee was named to review the needs of the university and the top priorities identified were capital projects and endowment, especially for student scholarships and faculty chairs.[28]

Laney condensed the report to one page with two columns, showing on the left column the capital needs and on the right column the endowment needs. Continuing his established practice of visiting Woodruff early in the late afternoon, Laney presented this report to Woodruff with two objectives in mind. "First, I wanted Mr. Woodruff to let us name him as the honorary chairman of the campaign. Second, I wanted to begin planting the seed of what he might do to assist us financially," Laney remembers.[29] Laney began with the second objective first and was shocked by the reaction. In reviewing the needs of the university, Woodruff commented that endowment was nothing more than "idle capital," and that he was not in favor of that. Laney left the visit dejected and fearful that the campaign prospects were all but lost because Woodruff was clearly the key to its success.

For days, Laney pondered how to handle this unexpected turn of events, and came up with the idea to change the title of the second column of the report from "Endowment"—which Woodruff interpreted as idle capital—to "Working Capital." Laney returned with the report unchanged, with the exception of the change in title. Woodruff's response was positive. Laney remembers Woodruff commenting that every institution needs "working capital," and so Woodruff gave his blessing to the campaign.[30] He agreed to be the honorary chair, but the financial support took a turn that no one expected, not even Woodruff.

Simultaneous to the relationship Laney was building with Woodruff and the plan Laney was making for Emory's first capital campaign in over a decade, the Woodruff brothers began to ask questions about how they should handle the Emily and Ernest Woodruff Fund, of which they were the trustees. As the corpus had grown to $100 million, and as the brothers were getting older, George especially worried that improper management of the fund after their deaths might bankrupt the fund. In its current form, the fund's proceeds were fixed with 40% per year going to Emory and the remaining 60% going to twenty-seven different entities.[31]

The original thinking about the Woodruff involvement in the campaign was proposed by Emory trustee and friend James Sibley. A partner in the Atlanta law firm of King and Spalding, Sibley suggested to the Woodruffs that they consider an increase in the payout of the Woodruff Fund to Emory from 40% to 60%, which would be a significant increase in income for Emory.[32] It was George Woodruff who had the idea to give the entire fund to Emory. George Woodruff said, "My brother and I talked about giving the assets of the foundation to Emory. His idea was to give part of it to Emory, and my idea was to give it all to Emory. And he finally agreed to that. I just figured the money would do more good."[33] So, in an ironic twist, the brother least courted by Laney had the idea to be the most generous. Still, the elder Woodruff's blessing was essential, and there is no doubt that the confidence he had in Laney's leadership, as the result of Laney's strategic cultivation of him, proved propitious. Thus, the Woodruff gift to Emory demonstrated a truism of fund-raising that relationships and the timing of the asking for the gift are paramount.

At the 1979 fall meeting of the Emory board, trustee George Woodruff had the honor of reading a letter from his brother officially announcing the gift, portions of which said:

> Gratified by Emory's progress, its demonstrated capacity to manage its affairs, and its continued commitment to educational excellence in the service of society, trustees of the Emily and Ernest Woodruff Fund have determined that resources committed to their care for public benefit can be of greatest potential for service in the South, their area of special interest, if concentrated now in Emory University.
>
> After fulfilling all commitments through 1979 and subject to appropriate governmental approval, the Emily and Ernest Woodruff Fund, Inc. will transfer to Emory University early in 1980 all of its net assets, valued in excess of $100,000,000, to be retained as a seperate [sic] endowment with income to be used for purposes of the university as determined by its board of trustees.[34]

On this day, the nation and the world came to know the name of Emory University, as news of the gift, the largest ever in philanthropy, made headlines everywhere. The $160 million capital campaign publicly announced that day was well over one-half way toward its goal, and overnight the Emory endowment increased from $175 million to $280 million, making it the thirteenth largest endowment among higher education institutions in the US.[35] Laney had succeeded not only in securing Emory's largest gift ever, but in seeing that it was given for unrestricted purposes that could benefit the entire university, rather than for the medical school exclusively, which had historically been the brothers' principal financial interest.

With the gift committed, Laney and his colleagues were faced with the decision of how to use the funds. Knowing several months in advance of the official announcement of the gift that was coming Emory's way, Laney began mulling his options. The first consideration was whether the income from the endowment could be used for the regular operating budget. Convinced that this approach could diminish the impact the gift would have on the whole of Emory, Laney determined that the endowment should function, instead, as an in-house foundation. He conveyed this desire to the Woodruff brothers in advance of the announcement, and they set the terms of the gift such that it be used strictly for endowment purposes.[36]

In describing to the Emory faculty how the gift would be used, Laney said that the endowment would be dedicated to helping the university achieve new levels of excellence and achievement. He went on to say that the budget for the upcoming year had been set without any reliance on the Woodruff funds, so as to force the university to be clear about what it needed.[37] For the short-term, individual faculty and divisions were invited to submit proposals for visiting professorships, faculty research and leaves, junior faculty development, and special one-time needs. Faculty were told that these proposals would be "as carefully screened as proposals received by any major foundation in America."[38]

To determine the steps the university should take to achieve excellence, Laney invited the "vigorous participation" of the faculty in this process. He directed every division and unit of the University to undergo an internal review over the next nine months. The review was to include those particular needs of the department/division, but "should examine as well its relation to the University as a whole."[39] Faculty were told that these reports would be turned over to an external review team to be headed by Dean Howard Lamar of Yale College. He, along with four visiting academicians, would be "charged with integrating the reports, assessing the long-term goals of the divisions, consulting with academic officers and making recommendations to the administration."[40]

Laney also announced to the Emory faculty that a portion of the endowment would be dedicated to meeting some of the critical needs identified for the campaign, namely full-tuition scholarships for students and endowed faculty positions, all to bear the name of Woodruff. The Woodruff Scholars would be "selected solely on merit, with leadership potential, academic ability, and character as the chief criteria for selection and the aim of developing leaders to serve Georgia, the South, and the nation."[41] Five Woodruff Professorships would be filled in the next year, faculty were told, with the intent of attracting persons of international renown. A Woodruff Advisory Committee of tenured faculty from across the university was named to review internal recommendations of who should be recruited for these positions.[42] Laney concluded his four page memorandum to the faculty about the importance of the gift and the opportunity before Emory in this way:

> It should be clear that the critical factor in this program
> of general assessment lies in the degree to which you and
> your colleagues join in this evaluation with critical rigor,
> imagination, and ambition....As we seek to strengthen
> our own programs the challenge to us all is to range
> beyond our separate fields by participating in the "inter-
> migration of disciplines and ideas," to use the words of
> Chicago's William Rainey Harper. In the process, I trust,

we will not only build a finer University but develop a
more creative, gracious community.[43]

Laney's reference to Harper in this communication, no doubt, signaled
his own belief that Emory had before it an opportunity not unlike that
Harper faced some ninety years prior, namely to build a university of the
first rank.

The delay of the use of the income from the endowment provided a
substantial reserve on which the university could undertake much needed capital projects. These projects—already identified by the Priorities
Review Committee—included a new gymnasium, a student life center,
new dormitories and upgrading of old ones.[44] Monies were also made
available for faculty research (approximately $300,000), library support
(approximately $172,000), visiting professors (approximately $287,000),
and plant and equipment (approximately $246,000). Within five years
the amounts for annual library support increased significantly to
$450,000.[45]

In addition to the projects undertaken with Woodruff endowment
income, Laney rallied the support of many both inside and outside the
university to assist in the reinventing of Emory as a first-rank institution.
Internally, Laney invited faculty to have a say in what the gift could mean
to their departments. Faculty chaired every review committee, giving
them a sense of ownership in the future of the institution. This helped to
overcome restlessness on the part of faculty, some of whom felt that the
university had been adrift until this point.[46] One example of the value of
involving the faculty was a recommendation from them that small portions of the endowment's earnings be used to separate the anthropology
and sociology department from each other. This move provided a freedom to anthropology that enabled it to flourish to the point of becoming
a nationally ranked program in less than a decade.[47]

Externally, Laney shared the internal findings with a review team of distinguished faculty from across the country that he hand picked. Included on the team was Dr. Howard Lamar as chairman; Dr. Stanley Cavell—a philosopher from Harvard; Dr. Robert Bellah—a sociologist from the University of California, Berkeley; Dr. Eliot Stellar—a physicist and the provost of the University of Pennsylvania; Dr. Maurice Glicksman—a biologist and the provost of Brown; and Dr. Judith Shklar—a professor of government and feminist scholar from Harvard.[48] Laney chose scholars, then, from some of the country's leading institutions. By tapping into the expertise of recognized scholars and administrators from diverse disciplines, serving at leading research institutions, Emory had the benefit of both educating these authorities about the possibilities at Emory, and, thereby gaining more recognition for Emory, and of receiving thoughtful advice about how to become a university of the first rank. Although not conscious of it, Laney was replicating a practice undertaken by Rockefeller when he determined that he wanted to found a new university. He listened to the voices of many people, including leaders in the Baptist church, the foundation world, Chicago business, and higher education. It was Rockefeller's consultations with Harper, who, at the time, was at Yale, that proved to be most influential in his thinking and, ultimately, his hiring of Harper to carry out his and Harper's dream.[49]

The external review team, which became known as the Lamar Committee, began its meetings in early 1981, with a meeting nearly every two months in the first year, twice per year in years two and three, and once per year in years four and five before the group was disbanded. The team was given carte blanche to explore any facet of the university. The team interviewed faculty, students, administrators, including notable personalities from the days of the "old Emory." It toured facilities, including dormitories and food service areas. The review was in every respect comprehensive, intended to aid Emory in its unique opportunity because of the Woodruff legacy to reinvent itself.[50]

The very definite feedback of the review team was that Emory need-ed to take immediate measures to strengthen its graduate program, for it was "perhaps the last private university in the United States to have ade-quate resources to set a new course for graduate education,"[51] an approach reminiscent of Harper's insistence that Chicago would become great because of its attention to graduate education and research.[52] One member of the committee wrote in this regard, "A major improvement in graduate education and in research faculty is the best way to improve all aspects of the University, to affect its entire intellectual spirit for the bet-ter."[53] The team especially hoped that the university would make a substantive commitment to the dimension of ethics and values, alongside an emphasis on cross-disciplinary and integrated research. The specific disciplinary recommendations included a strengthening of the physics department, giving greater attention to the sociology department, adding an art museum, and separating economics from the business division so that economic theory could be addressed. It was also suggested because of the competitive environment from public institutions that attention be given to whether the university should continue to support the geol-ogy department, the dental school, and the library science program. Each of the team's recommendations was accepted, and after thorough study geology, dentistry (except for postdoctoral work), and library science were eliminated.[54]

The team suggested that Emory's future prominence would depend upon using monies to recruit new faculty talent, including women and minorities, especially at the junior and associate level, with this logic gov-erning their view: "Senior people can be magnates and leaders, but for the long haul (e.g., 2000 AD), it will be the Assistant Professors and young Associate Professors who will carry Emory to its high goals. Therefore, a large proportion of the Woodruff Endowment funds should go to the support of the best young people."[55] The committee cautioned that those recruited should be promised adequate research funding, in the neighborhood of $25,000 annually per professor. By 1986, Emory was putting over $500,000 annually into its Woodruff Professorships.[56]

Included in the proposals from the review team was the expectation that full tuition scholarships would be made available to students so as to "attract excellent graduate students as well as a more diverse undergraduate body."[57] Altogether, the university made thirty-six Woodruff Fellowships per year available to the graduate school, college, and professional schools. These awards provided full tuition and a stipend, and by 1986 Emory was devoting nearly $1.8 million to this program.[58] Over $50,000 per year was allocated to bring in large groups of prospective students to interview for the fellowships, with the idea that those not offered a Woodruff Fellowship would attend anyway, but with lesser awards.[59]

Given the opportunity Emory had to add new departments and centers to strengthen its academic programs, the review team offered this concluding caution: "…the task of the Emory Administration…is to establish a rational relation between the Divisions and Centers and between them and the entire University. This is where the boldness and uniqueness of the whole Emory thrust will make its mark in American higher education."[60] The team was very definitely impressed with the attention to the interdisciplinary opportunities not undertaken by other institutions, especially at the graduate level, that members believed would make Emory unique. In the early years following the gift, Emory directed $250,000 annually for the Center for Public Policy, $30,000 annually for the International Studies Center, $40,000 for the Rollins Center for Church Ministries, and $100,000 per year for the Center for Faith Development.[61] Although lodged in specific schools, these programs were interdisciplinary in approach, attracting faculty and student participation from throughout the university.

As Laney indicated in an address to the Southeastern Council on Foundations, the Woodruff gift provided Emory with the "margin of excellence" it needed. The opportunity to build key facilities, recruit strong academic leadership in the faculty, and recruit bright students gave Emory a sense of direction and purpose—a "future of promise," as Laney described it.

The gift had also inspired others to be financially supportive. Alumni giving in the year after the gift increased over 100 percent in amount of dollars given and the number of people giving. Instead of having a chilling effect on fund-raising, the Woodruff gift was a catalyst for others to contribute, such that the $160 million capital campaign was successfully completed in 1984 with $225 million in gifts and pledges.[62] Similarly, the initial Rockefeller gift of $600,000 on which Chicago was founded was matched with $400,000 from Chicagoans and Baptists to provide the necessary funding from which the university could begin its operation.[63]

The Woodruff gift of $105 million in 1979 was an historic moment in American philanthropy and, most certainly, in the life of Emory and the presidency of Laney. The gift came as the result of years, even decades, of cultivation of one of Atlanta's most prominent families. Once the gift was received in 1980, Emory entered into a period of intentional self-analysis at the behest of Laney. This review, critiqued by noted scholars throughout the country, provided a blueprint for Emory to follow that helped it emerge from its comfortable regional stature to become a major national research university.

---

[1]James L. Fisher and James V. Koch, *Presidential Leadership: Making a Difference* (Phoenix: Oryx Press, 1996) 347.

[2]Hugh Hawkins, *Between Harvard and America: The Educational Leadership of Charles W. Eliot* (New York: Oxford University Press, 1991) 170, 215.

[3]Frederick Rudolph, *The American College and University: A History* (New York: Alfred A. Knopf, Inc., 1983) 352.

[4]Mary Ann Dzuback, *Robert M. Hutchins: Portrait of an Educator* (Chicago: University of Chicago Press, 1991) 208–209.

[5]Wayne J. Urban, *Black Scholar: Horace Mann Bond 1904–1972* (Athens: University of Georgia Press, 1992) 113, 116, 143. It should be noted that much of the Rosenwald philanthropy was directed at Southern institutions, which Lincoln—located in Pennsylvania—was not. Urban notes that Bond was successful in securing a Ford Foundation grant while at Lincoln (p. 143).

[6]Nick Taylor, "Emory University on the Rise," *Atlanta Magazine* (May 1982): 74.

[7]James T. Laney, interview by author, tape recording, Emory University, Atlanta, 23 June 1998.

[8]Laney interview, 23 June 1998.

[9]"Emory Benefactor Accepts 37 Year-Old Honorary," *Emory Magazine* 55/3 (Fall Quarter 1979): 7. Also James T. Laney, interview by author, tape recording, Emory University, Atlanta, 11 November 1997. While Woodruff acceded to the awarding of the degree, he would only accept it if awarded in a private ceremony at his south Georgia plantation known as Ichauway, demonstrating his intense dislike for public functions and publicity.

[10]Laney interview, 11 November 1997.

[11]This tripartite relationship continues even today at Emory. During Laney's tenure, Laney served on the boards of both Coca-Cola and Trust Company Bank. Roberto Goizeuta, the chief executive officer of Coca-Cola, and Robert Strickland, the chief executive officer of Trust Company, served on Emory's board, with Strickland serving as chairman for the majority of Laney's tenure at Emory.

[12]Taylor, "Emory University on the Rise," 76.

[13]Taylor, "Emory University on the Rise," 76.

[14]Robert W. Woodruff to Bishop Arthur J. Moore, 5 November 1977, Robert W. Woodruff Alpha Files, box 85, folder 4, RWWL. In this letter, Woodruff urged that in his place be elected C. E. Thwaite, Jr., president of the Trust Company of Georgia.

[15]Department chairs to Charles Howard Candler, 3 April 1957, Bowden Papers, RWWL.

[16]Henry Bowden, interview by author, tape recording, Emory University, Atlanta, 2 March 1995.

[17]Arthur J. Moore to Robert W. Woodruff, 7 November 1957, Robert W. Woodruff Alpha Files, box 85, folder 4, RWWL.

[18]Robert W. Woodruff to Henry L. Bowden, 5 October 1976, Robert W. Woodruff Alpha Files, box 34, folder 13, RWWL. For a review of the historical influence of funders in the selection of academic presidents see chapter 1.

[19]Laney interview, 11 November 1997.

[20]Laney interview, 23 June 1998. Laney believes that the reason Woodruff could not refer to him as "Jim" is because of the awe he had of the office of president, instilled in him by events with President Dickey at Emory College in 1908 and 1909.

[21]James T. Laney to Robert W. Woodruff, 22 December 1977, Robert W. Woodruff Alpha Files, box 85, folder 6, RWWL.

[22]"Alistair Cooke's Visit," *Emory Magazine* 54/1 (Winter Quarter 1978): 12.

[23]Laney interview, 11 November 1977.

[24]Prayer Offered at the Birthday Dinner of Mr. Robert W. Woodruff, 6 December 1978, Robert W. Woodruff Alpha Files, document case 10, box "L," folder "Laney," RWWL.

[25]Laney interview, 23 June 1998.

[26]Boisfeuillet Jones to Robert W. Woodruff, 11 April 1978, Robert W. Woodruff Alpha Files, box 85, folder "Emory 1976–1985," RWWL.

[27]In an article about Emory written for the *Chronicle of Higher Education* ten years after the Woodruff gift, the author notes that even then among the prized possessions in Laney's office was a photograph of Laney and Woodruff together at Laney's inauguration. The writer describes the photograph in this way, "Robert Woodruff has his hand on Mr. Laney's shoulder, almost in an act of paternal benediction. 'To my friend, Dr. Laney, with affection and all good wishes,' it says." See Liz McMillen, "Transformation of Emory: A Small Atlanta Institution Is Using a Historic Gift to Vault Into Big-Time Ranks," *Chronicle of Higher Education* 26/4 (27 September 1989): A36. In an interview, Laney acknowledged that he sought in Woodruff the affection and approval he seldom received from his father (Laney interview, 23 June 1998).

[28]"Report of the Advisory Committee for Evaluation of Emory's Capital Needs," 26 February 1979, Laney Papers, box 4, RWWL.

[29]Laney interview, 23 June 1998.

[30]Laney interview, 23 June 1998.

[31]Taylor, "Emory University on the Rise," 73.

[32]James Sibley, interview by author, note recording, Atlanta, 14 July 1998.

[33]Taylor, "Emory University on the Rise," 73.

[34]Robert W. Woodruff to James T. Laney, not dated, Robert W. Woodruff Papers, collection 10, box 7, folder 2, RWWL. The total gift, as noted earlier, came to $105 million.

[35]Laney interview, 11 November 1977; Taylor, "Emory University on the Rise," 74.

[36]Taylor, "Emory University on the Rise," 74.

[37]James T. Laney to the Faculties of Emory University, 13 March 1980, Laney Papers, box 22, folder "Woodruff Foundation," RWWL.

[38]James T. Laney to the Faculties of Emory University, Laney Papers, 1.

[39]James T. Laney to the Faculties of Emory University, Laney Papers, 2.

[40]James T. Laney to the Faculties of Emory University, Laney Papers, 3.

[41]James T. Laney to the Faculties of Emory University, Laney Papers, 4.

[42]James T. Laney to the Faculties of Emory University, Laney Papers, 3–4.

[43]James T. Laney to the Faculties of Emory University, Laney Papers, 4.

[44]"Dr. Laney's Notes from His Speech at the Southeastern Council on Foundations," 29 October 1981, Laney Papers, box 25-2, folder "Speaking Engagements 1985–86," RWWL, 1.

[45]"Emory University, Emily and Ernest Woodruff Endowment Fund Income Utilized for Enrichment Purposes 1981–82 through 1986–87," no date, Laney Papers, box 16-2, folder "Five Year Plan," RWWL.

[46]"Speech at Southeastern Council on Foundations," 2.

[47]Billy E. Frye, interview by author, 23 June 1998, tape recording, Emory University, Atlanta.

[48]Dr. Howard Lamar, interview by author, tape recording, LaGrange GA, 9 July 1998. Lamar provided the names of these committee members, including their disciplines and institutional affiliations.

[49]Storr, Harper's University, 7–34.

[50]Lamar interview.

[51]McMillen, "Transformation of Emory," A36–37.

[52]Laurence Veysey, The Emergence of the American University (Chicago: University of Chicago Press, 1965) 376. He writes, "…graduate work was given great prominence at Chicago from the very first, and Harper promoted research with undeniable zeal, even proposing the endowment of 'research' professorships whose occupants would be freed from ordinary teaching duties."

[53]"Lamar Report: General Recommendations," 8 April 1982, Laney Papers, box 4/5, folder "Lamar Report," RWWL, 1 (hereafter, "Lamar Report").

[54]Lamar interview. For additional information on the demise of the three departments see pages 144-45.

[55]"Lamar Report," 5.

[56]"Woodruff Endowment Fund Income."

[57]"Lamar Report," 7.

[58]"Woodruff Endowment Fund Income."

[59]"Speech at Southeastern Council on Foundations," 2.

[60]"Lamar Report," 9.

[61]"Woodruff Endowment Fund Income."

[62]"Speech at Southeastern Council Foundations," 2.

[63]Richard Storr, *Harper's University: The Beginning* (Chicago: University of Chicago Press, 1966) 40.

PHOTO ALBUM

President Jimmy Carter and James Laney at groundbreaking for William R. Cannon Chapel, where Carter was also awarded the LL.D., 10 August 1979 (Office of University Photography, Emory University).

Robert Strickland (Chairman BOT), Jimmy Carter, and James Laney at news conference announcing Carter's relationship to Emory as professor and the establishment of the Jimmy Carter Center, 1982 (Office of University Photography, Emory University).

Berta and James Laney at reception for graduates and their families,
1984 (Office of University Photography, Emory University).

James Laney and George Woodruff at celebration of Woodruff's 90th birthday, 1985 (Office of University Photography, Emory University).

James Laney at Lullwater Day, 1985 (Office of University Photography, Emory University).

James Laney speaking at Emory Sesquicentennial celebration, 1986 (Office of University Photography, Emory University).

Emory mascot, Dooley, handing off torch to James Laney to signify beginning of Sesquicentennial Celebration, 1986 (Office of University Photography, Emory University).

Archbishop Desmund Tutu and James Laney, Commencement 1988 (Office of University Photography, Emory University).

James Laney and students, 1990 (Office of University Photography, Emory University).

Eduard Shevardnadze (then former minister of foreign affairs, USSR) and James Laney, Commencement 1991 (Office of University Photography, Emory University).

James Laney and Robert W. Woodruff at Laney's inauguration, 1978 (Emory Picture Collection, Emory University Archives, Robert W. Woodruff Library, Emory University).

Henry Bowden (chairman of BOT), James Laney, portrait of Robert W. Woodruff, at press conference announcing $105 million gift by Robert and George Woodruff, 1979 (Emory Picture Collection, Emory University Archives, Robert W. Woodruff Library, Emory University).

James Laney with trustees and administrators, 1982 (Emory Picture Collection, Emory University Archives, Robert W. Woodruff Library, Emory University).

James Laney at surprise celebration commemorating his tenth anniversary as president, 1987 (Emory Picture Collection, Emory University Archives, Robert W. Woodruff Library, Emory University).

James Laney, Jacque de Baerst (Belgian Consul General in Atlanta), and Ted Johnson (Director of Robert W. Woodruff Library), at reception commemorating the addition of the 2 millionth volume to the Robert W. Woodruff Library, 1987 (Emory Picture Collection, Emory University Archives, Robert W. Woodruff Library, Emory University).

Robert Strickland (chairman of BOT), Dominique de Menil
(Philanthropist, Patron of the Arts), Mikhail Gorbachev (former president
of the USSR), Jimmy Carter, and James Laney, Commencement 1992
(Emory Picture Collection, Emory University Archives, Robert W.
Woodruff Library, Emory University).

Farewell reception for James and Berta Laney as he leaves to become US Ambassador to South Korea, 1993 (Emory Picture Collection, Emory University Archives, Robert W. Woodruff Library, Emory University).

CHAPTER FOUR

THE LANEY YEARS

*Emory's Transformation from Regional Teaching University
to Major National Research University*

The Emory University that Laney inherited in 1977 was ready for new leadership. The departure of Laney's predecessor had been anticipated for two years, and the cynicism amongst faculty and students about the lack of progress Emory was making was heavy. Laney remembers that early in his presidency, he could not walk from his office to the cafeteria without encountering students who boldly told the new president all that was wrong with student life and academics and needed fixing. Students did not feel their presence was taken seriously by the administration. Laney knew early on he would need to make substantive changes and improvements.[1] By the time of his departure in 1993, there was no doubting that the changes Laney had wrought had made the institution much stronger and more nationally recognized.

Comparison of Emory's progress during the Laney era to institutions of the past is difficult because of institutional challenges unique to Emory and the era of 1977 to 1993. One significant similarity is worth noting, however, and that is the recognition by Laney that for Emory to achieve preeminence a strengthening of the graduate program would have to occur. This pattern was established early on by Harvard, Johns Hopkins, and Chicago, which made their graduate programs a priority. Harvard, for instance, became a university under Eliot's tenure, and he credited the new program at Johns Hopkins for the development at Harvard. In

1902, Eliot said: "The graduate school of Harvard University…did not thrive, until the example of Johns Hopkins forced our Faculty to put their strength into the development of our institution for graduates. And what was true of Harvard was true of every other university in the land which aspired to create an advanced school of arts and sciences."[2] Harper followed suit at Chicago in 1892 by making graduate work prominent from the beginning.[3]

In the development of graduate education at Emory, the desire to emulate and surpass the competition, as Harvard did with Hopkins, becomes very evident as Laney begins to compare Emory's progress with that of other private universities. In this way, Emory was still similar to the aspirations of the earliest universities in its desire to grow, expand, and become preeminent. Rudolph describes the phenomenon, "The developing universities revealed an appetite for expansion, a gluttony for work, a passion for growth which constituted one of their most fundamental characteristics."[4] What can be said of Emory's development during the period 1977 to 1993 is that the characteristics of growth, competition, and development of the graduate program were very much in evidence, and, in this respect, the achievements of Emory during this time make it a fascinating case study of development and transformation in higher education in the latter twentieth century. The distinctive character that Laney brought to this transformation was the insistence that Emory would be defined as a moral community, where issues of the common good and service to society would be paramount.[5] Evidence of this focus can be found in all three phases of Laney's administration.

Emory University History Prior to 1977

Billy E. Frye, provost of Emory during the latter part of Laney's administration, describes Emory as having three distinct epochs or eras since its founding as a university in 1915. The Laney era of 1977–1993 marks the beginning of the third epoch, a time when the "Woodruff Endowment and [Laney's] ambitious and enlightened leadership...gave [Emory] the privilege and responsibility of emerging preeminen[t]."[6] The challenges that Laney inherited were actually put in motion in 1915, the beginning of the first epoch, when the university was established. While the college, located in Oxford, Georgia, was identified as the core of the new university, the reality is that professional education dictated the agenda of the university. Even before Emory could be chartered as a university, the Candler School of Theology was started in a church. It was not until 1919, four years after the founding of the university, that Emory College would be relocated from Oxford to Atlanta. By then, the Candler School of Theology and the Atlanta Medical School, acquired by Emory in 1915, as well as the Lamar School of Law begun in 1916, had taken up residence on the Druid Hills campus.[7] As Emory grew, there seemed ambivalence about the core of the university, while the entrepreneurial instincts of presidents and board members led to the establishment of more professional divisions. The net effect of this growth was a "disconnected relationship among Emory's individual schools...and an ambiguous status of the arts and sciences, vis-a-vis the professional schools, in the overall mission and character of Emory."[8]

Frye's view concurs with Levine's contention about Emory during this time. Levine argues that the growth of Emory between 1915 and 1940 is prototypical of the secular and urban influences that brought about significant changes in higher education nationwide. The growth of the South and the need for a more professionally educated labor force resulted in a proliferation of professional programs at places like Emory.[9] Thus, by 1940, Emory had six professional schools (medicine, nursing, business, theology, law, and library science) in addition to the college, the graduate school (which offered only masters' degrees), and two junior colleges.[10]

The second epoch, following World War II and shared by most American universities, was a period of growth in enrollment, faculty, facilities, and the development of the Ph.D. program, with the first degree awarded in chemistry in 1948. While this set the stage for Emory's emergence as a national research university, social problems facing the South coupled with a "combination of inadequate means and perhaps some lack of consensus about the vision, [meant that] Emory's star lagged behind as others' rose."[11] Still, a core of mediocre to solid professional schools made Emory a solid regional teaching institution by 1977.[12]

The Laney Years, Phase One, 1977–1980

During his first three years in office, Laney spent time determining and refining his vision for Emory, conveying that vision to the various constituents of the university. He also identified the specific needs of the university, setting in motion a fund-raising plan to fulfill the vision and meet the needs, cultivating some of Emory's donors—especially Woodruff, reining in the financial fortunes of the medical center, and attempting to make the university more collegial for faculty. By the time Laney was named president, Emory had six professional schools, two divisions, the graduate school, the college, and Emory at Oxford—a junior college.[13] Of the 7,572 students enrolled in all programs in the fall of 1977, only 43 percent were enrolled in the college or Emory at Oxford.[14]

According to data supplied by the Cooperative Institutional Research Program (CIRP), of those enrolled in the college or Emory at Oxford well over one-half were preparing for professional education. Forty percent claimed to be pre-medicine, while 17 percent were pre-law, with both categories considerably above the national averages of 21 percent and 14 percent respectively.[15] Thus, the interest of many undergraduates was not on the liberal arts, but on pre-professional learning.

Furthermore, although the student population was geographically diverse with 45 percent of the students coming from outside the South, Laney was bothered that the brightest and best of Georgia were choosing to attend elsewhere. "The only reason bright Georgia students came to Atlanta," Laney said, "was to change airplanes at the Atlanta airport on their way to distinguished schools in the northeast." Thus, as Laney told the board of trustees in his first official meeting with them in 1977, he wanted to make sure "that Atlanta had a university worthy of the city."[16] Laney began his presidency by focusing his energies on the college, which he believed to be the core of the university.

In addition to the students who were bold to approach Laney early in his presidency about their complaints, he was aided in his knowledge of the issues confronting Emory students by himself being the parent of three Emory students who graduated in the years 1979, 1980, and 1983. While Laney does not credit his children's experience as having much impact on his knowledge of the problems at Emory, key administrators who worked with him believe that his children's experience provided an invaluable lens through which to gauge the problems and progress of the university.[17]

Armed with the data he had on the college and what he knew from the experience of his children, Laney identified early on curricular and capital challenges that had to be confronted to provide the foundation to strengthen the college and build a first-rate graduate program. Despite the deficits and challenges, Laney set as his goal for Emory membership in the Association of American Universities (AAU). To achieve this distinction enrollment in the college would have to increase to about 4,000 per year from the current 2,700 and the number of Ph.D. graduates from seventy per year to 100 per year. Likewise, the graduate program would have to improve so that it was built on "solid research, a top faculty, and the best students."[18]

Laney's strategy of making the liberal arts program of the college and the graduate school a priority would, he believed, be the key to the internal strengthening of the total university. Laney said:

> ...the whole liberal arts program, if you include under-
> graduate and graduate, was very weak relative to the
> other parts of the university, and particularly the medical
> school. And I didn't want to do anything at the medical
> school's expense. I just wanted to strengthen what I felt
> was the heart of the university. There is no conceivable
> way to have a great university without a great liberal arts
> program. So, when I became president, that became my
> passion, to strengthen the college.[19]

Laney was convinced that for graduate education to flourish, an increase would be required in the enrollment of the undergraduate population, but he did not want the increase in enrollment at the expense of quality. So, he set as lofty goals an increase both in the number and quality of undergraduates. This goal was made even more difficult by the limited resources the university was devoting to financial aid. The total financial aid budget in 1977 was less than $1 million.[20] Before 1979, the college offered only twenty-three scholarships, totaling no more than $500 each.[21]

In a faculty meeting in February 1978, Laney gave a "State of Emory Address," discussing how he saw the institution. He identified pressing needs, such as increased scholarships for students and salaries for faculty. He noted problems with affirmative action policies, safety on Clifton Road—the main corridor through Emory, and fire and security precautions in the dormitories. The main focus of his address, however, was his concern about the future of Emory and the need to determine the nature of an Emory education, the quality of research, and the kind of student life Emory wanted to provide.[22]

To identify key objectives for Emory's future, Laney informed the faculty he was naming the Advisory Committee for the Evaluation of Emory's Capital Needs to ascertain priorities and needs of the University. All this was a precursor to a capital campaign, as the last fund-raising effort had been nearly a decade ago. In this same presentation, Laney embarked on a detailed presentation to the audience about the university's budget, the size of the endowment, and the relative financial strengths of the various schools of Emory.[23]

In his conclusion, Laney called on his colleagues to participate in the determination of Emory's vision. He reminded the audience that an educational institution is like a living organism, where concern for the health and well-being of all must be practiced. He noted that a certain level of trust would be necessary to fulfill the vision and that instead of an attitude of an expert—such as "'I know better than you.'"—Emory would need to practice "collegial delegation."[24] This set the stage for some of the developments that occurred at Emory until 1980.

In early 1979, the Advisory Committee for the Evaluation of Emory's Capital Needs submitted its report to Laney on the pressing needs facing the university. The committee included a cross-section of faculty and staff from throughout the university. Its deliberations occurred over eleven meetings, and included the feedback of faculty, students, non-faculty employees, and alumni. The report identified in excess of $200 million worth of need. Endowment for scholarships, faculty, library, and programs was given the highest priority. Capital needs were also identified, with strong emphasis placed on the need for a physical education building and a student center.[25]

These needs were presented to the board of trustees, and a capital campaign was approved at the spring 1979 meeting to raise $160 million. Trustee and alumnus, Jimmy Williams, the chief executive officer of Trust

Company Bank, was the chairman of the fund-raising effort, with Robert Woodruff serving as the honorary chairman. Although the campaign was not concluded until well into the second phase of Laney's administration in 1984, the campaign was successfully completed with $225 million raised.[26]

In addition to the Woodruff gift of $105 million, trustees and administrators who worked with Laney consider another great accomplishment of the first phase of Laney's presidency to be the way he handled the challenges of the Emory Clinic doctors. Since the early 1940s the Emory Clinic and hospitals had become powerhouses at Emory, thanks in large measure to the support of the Woodruff brothers. Doctors who saw patients in the clinic had faculty appointment in the medical school. Emory provided for these doctors the buildings and equipment to conduct their work, and, in return, the doctors paid a modest fee to the university for its support. Each year the fee paid was renegotiated and based on a percentage of the fair market value of the facilities and equipment. This arrangement worked fine, except Laney knew that the doctors were making substantial fortunes in the fees they charged. So that Emory might get a fairer share of support and increase its revenues from the clinic, Laney proposed, and eventually prevailed in having approved, a new and controversial formula for determining the fees. Laney wanted 10 percent of these revenues, which was substantially more than the doctors were paying under the old formula. The new formula also had the benefit of eliminating the contentiousness that occurred each year when the fair market value of facilities and equipment was determined.[27] Laney's success in these negotiations was seen as a huge breakthrough, since previously the clinic was viewed, for the most part, as independent, with little accountability to the larger university.[28]

Laney's attention in this first phase of his administration was not devoted solely to budgetary and fund-raising matters. He wanted also to strengthen faculty morale. Among the difficulties Laney inherited when he became president was the lack of communication and conversation that the faculty experienced with each other and with the administration.[29] To change this and create the community of scholars that was at the heart of his view of the liberal arts institution, Laney supported and backed with resources the suggestion of some Emory faculty to celebrate the fiftieth anniversary of the founding of a chapter of Phi Beta Kappa at Emory. The announcement about the symposium was made in late 1977, giving approximately eighteen months to undertake the planning. In his announcement, Laney offered the following observation about its value to Emory and the academy generally: "The spirit of such a celebration challenges this faculty, if it would take a step toward preeminence, to define and confront some of the major intellectual concerns that demand the Academy's attention today and in the future."[30] Thus, the stage was set to undertake a symposium that would benefit Emory and higher education generally.

For others in higher education to benefit from the symposium, Laney determined that the publication of the proceedings in *Daedalus* would be appropriate. An additional benefit of such a publication would be that Emory's name would be associated with the leading scholarly interdisciplinary journal in the country. Laney persuaded the editors of *Daedalus* that publication of the proceedings would be good for the journal, especially if Emory would provide the funding, and in the spring 1980 issue, the entire publication was devoted to the Emory symposium. In the preface to the issue, the editors had this to say about Laney and his role: "The funding for this issue came principally from Emory University. The role of President Laney in securing these funds—indeed, in seeing the possibility of such a mutually advantageous collaboration—cannot be too highly praised. We feel a deep gratitude to him."[31]

A large cross-section of Emory faculty served on the Presidential Planning Committee for the event. In addition to medicine, law, and theology, the disciplines of English, biochemistry, economics, anatomy, religion, sociology, classics and art history were represented in the planning. Finally the interdisciplinary topic of "Intellect and Imagination" was decided upon. Renowned faculty from around the country were chosen to present papers. Among the eight participants, three were from Harvard and one each was from Cornell, Brown, University of Pennsylvania, University of Chicago, and Stanford[32]—all schools with leading liberal arts programs with which Laney was eager to associate Emory.

In reflecting on the symposium, Laney described it as a highlight of his tenure at Emory. He said, "It was really, and I say this very, very rarely, a thrilling experience. I think for the first time a lot of my colleagues had a glimpse of what we could do together out of that."[33] By lifting up an interdisciplinary effort of this magnitude, Laney quieted some of his critics who feared that a clergyman and former theological dean would be too narrowly focused in his thinking about the role of the university. Instead, he showed that the life of the mind was for him a priority. Furthermore, the symposium gave evidence of his profound commitment to liberal arts education, and it provided occasion for a university-wide conversation about compelling intellectual issues.

Laney's success in conveying his vision for the future of Emory by getting support of the trustees for the capital campaign, and the early success of this effort with the gift of $105 million from the Woodruff brothers, brought to conclusion the first phase of his presidency and set the stage for the initiatives he would undertake in phases two and three. Also, Laney's appeal for faculty involvement and the success of the Phi Beta Kappa Symposium gave him a confidence in his relations with the faculty that enabled him to pursue with some vigor the challenges facing the college and the graduate school. The college and its students would take precedence in phase two.

The Laney Years, Phase Two, 1981–1986

Lack of funds and numerous pressing priorities prevented Laney from making substantive changes in the college and student life until after 1980. Even in an address to the faculty in 1982, Laney expressed his frustration with the slowness of change at Emory, especially given the resources at its disposal. He noted that he felt Emory faced two conundrums. The first conundrum was that there was not enough money to do all that was wanted, despite the enormous success of the campaign. As he said, we have "to reconcile success in the Campaign with the need to tighten our belts."[34] The second conundrum Laney expressed was that Emory was projecting an image of making success, but he (Laney) "didn't see it."[35] Especially disappointing to him was that the graduate school had not made more progress. He reiterated his concern to the gathering that no university can become great without a great graduate school. He also restated his intention to make the graduate school great by building it on the base of the college, which would have increased enrollment.[36] He concluded his presentation with a theme that he had expressed to the faculty on other occasions, namely that what would make Emory unique was the development of a human community, which represented "the human mind and spirit at their best."[37] In this second phase of Laney's administration, key administrative appointments and the use of Woodruff monies would leave no doubt that the build up of the college for the sake of a strong graduate program was Laney's top priority.

Among Laney's first significant administrative appointments was the hiring of Dr. David Minter as dean of the college in 1981. A member of the English faculty at Rice University, Minter and Laney had crossed paths briefly when they were both at Yale. Minter had attended the Yale Divinity School as well, but moved on to Yale's English program where he earned his Ph.D. The Woodruff gift had already been announced, and the potential for the use of the gift and the transformation that Minter believed it could bring to Emory to make it first-rank compelled him to accept the position.[38]

Minter remembers that the college was in a dismal state. College faculty had an attitude of resignation because they had for so long been ignored. The budget was "pathetic," and the college was accepting nearly 90 percent of the applicants, most of whom made Emory a second, third, or fourth choice, usually after having not been admitted to Ivy League institutions. All of this had to be changed. Minter credits Laney's understanding that a research university only becomes great when it has a great liberal arts program in the college as the vision necessary to provide the funding to make the college grow and flourish.[39]

Among the first things that Minter encouraged Laney to do was to make significant funds available for scholarships through the Woodruff gift. This was a controversial move because many faculty believed that the funds initially should be used to upgrade salaries, offices, and research budgets. But Minter's and Laney's wisdom was that if students were attracted to Emory, additional funds would flow into the institution such that these other matters would care for themselves. Beginning in 1981–1982, Laney agreed to the Minter proposal of $1.2 million in scholarships for entering students that year, and to the long range strategy of increasing that amount by $200,000 for each subsequent class, up to $1.8 million. The end result would be that the Woodruff Fellowships and other scholarships would serve as magnets for others to attend, with students of better quality, who were also more geographically and racially diverse. Also Emory would attract students for whom Emory was their first choice, and improve the retention rate, which in 1981 was at 60 percent.[40]

The effort to attract more students was modestly successful. By 1984, the total university enrollment was 8,533, up from 7,572 in 1977. Enrollment in the college in 1984 was up by just over 600 students from 1977, with an enrollment of 3,298.[41] By 1986, the scholarship budget was increased to over $20 million, which helped Emory in attracting these new students, who, overall, were of better quality.[42] In an address to the Emory Board of Visitors in 1986, Laney celebrated the fact that more students were coming to Emory from the South. In that year, 25 percent of the students were from Georgia, which was up from 18 percent when Laney became president in 1977. Laney expressed his satisfaction with the Georgia enrollment:

> We want the best students from throughout the South. We got tired of having students from Valdosta and Statesboro and Newnan, coming through Atlanta and changing planes and going up to Yale or Princeton or Harvard or Chicago, or wherever they went. We thought they ought to come to Atlanta and stay. And more and more they are beginning to do that.[43]

As the enrollment grew, and Laney placed more emphasis on the college, he knew that one area desperate for attention was the student life program. Complaints from students about the condition of facilities and the lack of caring attitude from administrators and faculty toward students were numerous. Laney took immediate steps to address this concern, changing the name of the office concerned with student matters from Student Life to Campus Life, eliminating the dean of men and dean of women positions, and creating a vice presidential level position for Campus Life, with an administrator empowered to address student needs and concerns. The first appointee to the post, hired after a nationwide search, proved ill-suited for the role, and Laney appointed Dr. William H. Fox—who was then director of Emory's Institute for the Liberal Arts—as interim, eventually elevating him to the post permanently.[44] Quickly, Fox set out to act on recommendations of the Advisory Committee for the Evaluation of Emory's Capital Needs that more facilities were needed to create a community for students and faculty. With the benefit of the Woodruff gift, a new gymnasium, student center, and dormitories were built in short order. Other steps were taken to develop a philosophy of student life that mirrored Laney's vision of a strengthened college. Included in that plan was an increase in staffing to tend to student concerns as they arose, with the establishment of offices for international students, students with disabilities, a multicultural center, a counseling center, and a gay/lesbian/bisexual life office. The plan also focused on enhancing student activities, including the establishment of the University Athletic Association (UAA),[45] which Emory was a key player in creating, and the development of outlets for students to show their concern for the world through organizations such as Volunteer Emory, AIDS Emory, and Habitat for Humanity.[46] Laney's pride in the progress of student services during this second phase of his administration was expressed at a 1987 trustee retreat in which he said: "…without any exception the life of the students on our campus is as good as any in the country in terms of the way it is organized and supported in the residence halls, and supplemented with the new athletic program and with Volunteer Emory."[47]

Among Laney's greatest preoccupations in the building up of the college was to foster a sense of moral community and to create a means by which students could enjoy the faculty mentor relationships that had been so important to him at Yale. Responding to Laney's vision for a vehicle for these mentor relationships to occur, the academic and campus life offices of the university worked together in the creation of the Freshman Seminar. The intent of the program was to divide entering students into small, diverse groups of eight students and assign each group to a faculty member and Emory staff person. The groups met weekly to read and discuss short, provocative works, such as Martin Luther King, Jr.'s "Letter from the Birmingham Jail." Students were required to take the class, for which they received credit and a grade. Out of these groupings it was hoped that students would experience what an "intellectual" community and a moral community of support were. Faculty leaders were the advisors to students in their group, thereby strengthening the advising function, which, up to that point, had been spotty, if not poor.[48] Among the comments Laney made about the program, this one is especially illuminating:

> Meeting weekly over the course of the year, these students and their mentors [faculty] come to know each other very well in the midst of the otherwise largely anonymous complex of the university.... Out of that experience may come, we hope, a substitute for an earlier, maybe more moralistic kind of monitoring process. What we are trying to do, in short, is to suggest that there are certain elements of civilized life that go with being in a university, and we want to elicit these in ways that are not hectoring, but are suggestive.[49]

The opinion of Minter and Fox is that the program, which continues even today, was largely successful and became a model for other higher education institutions because of its novel approach. Because of the sheer numbers of faculty and students involved in the experience, it was not uniformly positive for all. However, in general, it was seen as an important step in creating the moral community and faculty-student network about which Laney felt so powerfully.[50]

To keep pace modestly with the growth in enrollment during the second phase of Laney's administration, ninety-eight faculty appointments, some of them at the Woodruff Professorship level, were made for a net gain of fifty-three new faculty.[51] Yet, the enrollment growth was such that the new faculty appointments could not keep up. The faculty-student ratio increased, as did reliance on teaching assistants for introductory level courses. Minter was pleased, however, that the stature of the faculty was greatly improved as evidenced by the large number of offers Emory faculty were receiving from other institutions, reflecting the practice of raiding faculty at other institutions begun at Harvard, Chicago, and elsewhere in the late nineteenth century. Minter offered this observation to the trustees:

> Another sign of progress is the presence on our faculty of people who are being recruited by faculties of the most distinguished universities in the United States. I actually spend more of my time than I want to talk about trying to persuade faculty that in the long run they are better off here than at Stanford or UCLA or Berkeley or Northwestern.... Certainly it is a sign of the quality of our faculty...that we are now more and more under siege.[52]

The increased caliber of the faculty and the desire to become more nationally known resulted in new standards of evaluation for attainment of tenure. New tenure decision guidelines were adopted in 1981, stressing that research and publication would be valued equally highly as teaching. These new standards created tensions which would become more pronounced in the third phase of Laney's administration—about which more will be said later—but the concern, as expressed by Minter, was to deepen "the faculty's established tradition of fine teaching, on the one side, while intensifying an uneven tradition in scholarship and research, on the other."[53] The focus on research had shown some tangible results, according to Minter, of an average annual increase of $2 million in funded research in the college. From 1981 to 1986, funded research increased from $2.1 million to $14.5 million.[54]

Laney's greatest faculty coup of phase two was the luring of former US President Jimmy Carter to Emory as a University Distinguished Professor. Not only did this hiring bring significant international attention to Emory, but it placed in Emory's midst a world-known leader, who reflected with students on the state of affairs in the world. It also assured Emory's close tie to the Carter Library and Presidential Center. By virtue of his position, Carter was given the flexibility to lecture and teach in those parts of the university that interested him, and where he received invitations. In making the significant announcement of President Carter's appointment in 1982, Laney had this to say: "The presence of this former President of the United States, with his great intelligence, particular sensitivities, and unique fund of experiences, will prove to be an enormously valuable resource for our students and faculty. We are confident as well that he will find the challenge of academic life here refreshing and fulfilling."[55] In 1987, an issue of *Newsweek on Campus* had as its lead story the hiring of "superstar" faculty by college campuses. On the front cover was a picture of President Carter walking through the Rudolph Courtyard on the Emory campus surrounded by students and the press. The article said about Carter's value to Emory: "While his occasional classes are popular, Carter's chief value to the university is his ability to draw admissions and attention. '*The New York Times* used to refer to it as 'Emory University in Atlanta,' says a recent graduate Mark Joyella. 'Now it's just Emory.' They don't have to tell where it is."[56] In reflecting on his accepting the offer to come to Emory, Carter had this to say about the significance of Laney's role in his decision making:

> People often ask me why I came to Emory University. I invariably answer, "Jim Laney." In 1981, when Rosalynn and I were trying to decide what we should do with the rest of our lives, we had many attractive offers of employment. We chose Emory because Jim Laney convinced us

that he had a moral and ethical vision for the university that we could share and help to advance.[57]

By 1986, Laney shared with Emory's Board of Visitors that he believed Emory was making great strides and that this was recognized by Emory's being named as one of the twelve "hottest" colleges in the country.[58] Students were better appreciated and integrated into the life of the college by virtue of the Freshman Seminar, the new facilities, and the enhanced scholarship support they received. Jimmy Carter's joining the Emory faculty reinforced the perception in the higher education community that Emory was growing and changing. The base of the college was well in place and would continue to grow until 1993, but the progress of the graduate school and the support of faculty had been disappointing up to that point. The third phase of Laney's administration would attempt to address all of those concerns.

At the 1986 Board of Visitors meeting, Laney described Emory:

> ...we have over 8,000 students today.... They come from 50 states and 83 foreign countries. With 8,000 full-time employees, including 1,250 faculty, Emory is one of the largest employers in the metropolitan area....As of last August, Emory's total assets were right at one and a quarter billion dollars, half of which was in endowment; Emory's net worth is now almost a billion dollars. Our annual budget is now over 400 million dollars; and if you use the multiplier effect as they do downtown for conventioneers, we'd say that Emory contributes probably 1.2 billion dollars annually to the total economy of the metropolitan Atlanta....The great difference between Emory and the huge mega-universities with 20 to 50 thousand students is that at Emory we are trying

> to build a community—a community of learning and of
> character…. People who have a sense of service for soci-
> ety, that understand what citizenship is all about. People
> who give of themselves, who understand that real
> authority comes from giving more than you get.[59]

As the second phase of Laney's administration drew to a close and the
third phase began, Laney held that, along with the strides of the
University, at Emory's core remained a commitment to values and moral
concern.

The Laney Years, Phase Three, 1987–1993

The year 1987 marked the tenth anniversary of Laney's presidency
and the 150th anniversary of the founding of Emory. Both events proved
to be occasions for considerable reflection on from where Emory had
come and to where Emory should go. With the new millennium only
thirteen years away, Laney turned his thoughts to what Emory could do
to build on the momentum created by the developments of the first two
phases of his administration, so that Emory would emerge as a great
national research university in the third phase. With the build-up of the
college and the substantial improvements in campus life, Laney began to
press harder his vision, expressed from his arrival as president, that Emory
must have a strong graduate program. To achieve this would require a significant investment in the faculty, research budgets, and research
facilities. The goals Laney set out in 1987 in his Emory 2000 vision statement were virtually all achieved by the time he departed in 1993, a sign
of the enormous growth at Emory between 1987 and 1993.

In 1986, George Woodruff, the brother of Robert Woodruff, died
leaving an unrestricted bequest of nearly $25 million to Emory.[60] Laney's
dean of the graduate school, Billy Frye, saw an opportunity to put to use

a gift that could transform Emory's efforts in graduate education. In early 1987, Frye wrote to Laney urging that he consider something unique in higher education: to use the bequest entirely for the graduate program and to name the school for Woodruff. Frye believed that the earnings from the endowment would help Laney achieve all that he desired for the strengthening of the graduate program, which included:

> primary emphasis on student stipend support and improvement of quality; focus on a select number of central departments and programs with the goal of making a major move in these chosen areas; achieving a balance between support for traditional disciplines and the enhancement of important and novel cross-disciplinary graduate initiatives and, insofar as consistent with our academic goals, providing strong incentives to increase the level of external support for graduate students.[61]

Although Laney did not accept Frye's recommendation for the naming of the graduate school, he did agree with Frye's vision of what Emory needed in its graduate program. Thus, as Laney promoted his vision for Emory and its emphasis on graduate education, his descriptions broadened from Emory's being a university worthy of the city of Atlanta to one of a dozen elite private universities in the United States. He said he believed that Emory had been appropriately limiting in its thinking about itself up until then, measuring its progress based on its past, instead of benchmarking itself against a group of peer institutions. Now, though, had come the time for benchmarking and stretching even more. Laney expressed his conviction to the trustees in a 1987 retreat at Sea Island, Georgia, in this manner:

...up until this point in time, we at Emory have tended to measure ourselves against ourselves.... The great move I would hope we would acknowledge and accept at this retreat is that we begin to see ourselves in relationship to a specific peer group of institutions. We are now positioned...to aspire to be in a select group of leading private institutions in this nation—helping to set the pace for what goes on. Today south of the line that stretches from Baltimore to Los Angeles there is no University in that category.... This needs to be remedied. If nothing else I want to play on upon your sense of provincial loyalty and southern pride. It is intolerable that there is no educational institution in the southern tier of the United States that stands absolutely and unquestionably in that top tier of the twelve outstanding institutions.[62]

Laney's vision for Emory and the need to strengthen its graduate program was reinforced by a presentation later that day from Frye. He explained to the group that "graduate education is to the university and the life of scholarship as professional education is to the professions.... Graduate education lies so close to the heart of what a university is above all else, and that is a place where knowledge is pursued for its own sake."[63]

Building on Frye's earlier correspondence to him about the needs for the graduate school, Laney outlined for the trustees eleven goals he believed were necessary to achieve his vision. Among the eleven, three emerged as most central to his vision. First, Laney wanted to double the university's funded research base, which stood at about $50 million, by the year 2000. At that point in 1987, Emory was eighty-sixth in the nation in receipt of federal funds. By doubling research funding, Laney was confident that Emory could move into the top twenty-five, despite the absence of an engineering program, which for other institutions was key to their large research base. In making his point, Laney was unabashed in chiding those present, along with Emory graduates who were US senators from Georgia, that they had a moral obligation to make this happen. Laney argued:

> We have two senators in Washington, both of whom have Emory law degrees, and they need to take it to heart that last year Georgia received $6 per capita in research grants from the government while Connecticut and Massachusetts received over $60. That's a ten to one disparity. Now I can assure you that Sam Nunn would not tolerate a ten to one disparity between Massachusetts and Connecticut and Georgia in military appropriations. If Georgia is truly to emerge, it must to [sic] have the kind of high quality research work going on, and it befits Atlanta as a great city to have a great private university with a great research power base.[64]

A second goal of Laney's Emory 2000 vision was the need to increase the number of Ph.D. graduates from approximately seventy per year to over 100 per year. Only by increasing the number of Emory doctoral graduates in teaching and research could Emory begin to establish the reputations enjoyed by Yale, Harvard, Stanford, and Chicago. As Frye noted to the group in his remarks about graduate education, very few members of the AAU graduated fewer than 100 Ph.D.s per year.[65]

A third goal Laney identified was the commitment to an education focused on value and the moral development of students. For Laney, this focus would finally make Emory distinctive. A focus on service and not on self should be the hallmark of an Emory education. Laney knew that to do this would be difficult, and he admitted this in his remarks to the trustees by saying:

> So what I am proposing is the most difficult of all possi-
> ble worlds: namely that Emory continue to cling and
> embellish its heritage and be proud of it; that it's [sic]
> role includes the spiritual and character formation of its
> students; that it should articulate what that means for
> higher education while, at the same time, emerging as a
> principal player among the most select and distinguished
> universities in this country.[66]

While Laney was successful in securing the blessing and backing of trustees and faculty for his Emory 2000 vision, everyone was aware that the costs would be enormous. Although generously endowed, Emory needed new sources of funding, as the Woodruff gift was fully commit-ted. Thus, only five years after the last campaign, Emory embarked on another campaign, this one to raise $400 million. A review committee was established to determine the needs of the university, keeping in mind Laney's goals. Once the needs and dollar amounts had been tabulated, the needs exceeded $1 billion. Fund-raising counsel made it clear that at most the university could hope to raise $400 million, and even that was considered difficult. Still, the trustees signed on for the five-year cam-paign in 1989, with Bradley Currey the campaign chairman and O. Wayne Rollins—one of Emory's most generous benefactors—the hon-orary chairman. In preparing board chairman Robert Strickland for a capital campaign, Laney stated the need: "The task ahead of us is to make the kind of long-term investments that will mean the most—to create the programs, build the labs, endow the scholarships necessary to sustain the university we want Emory to become, even though we may not live to see the results of our investment."[67] Laney would leave Emory before the campaign was concluded in 1995, but the campaign exceeded its $400 million goal.

Although the campaign would be a major preoccupation during the third phase of Laney's administration, emphasis still had to be placed on the college, especially student and faculty recruitment, if Emory was to achieve its goal of emerging as a major national research university. During the third phase, student enrollment had its greatest growth. Whereas college enrollment was 2,687 in 1977 and 3,298 in 1984, it grew to 4,473 in 1992.[68] The quality of students improved as well, with the average SAT score increasing from 1138 in 1984 (the first year Emory began collecting these data) to 1204 in 1992. Correspondingly, the average grade point average of enrollees increased from 3.4 in 1984 to 3.6 in 1992.[69] The freshmen enrollment became more diverse between 1977 and 1992, with white students declining from 95 percent to 78 percent. Between 1984 and 1992, African-American students increased from 3 to 9 percent, and Asian-Americans increased from 2 to 9 percent. Between 1977 and 1992, the percentage of freshmen from the South decreased from 55 to 47 percent, from the Middle Atlantic States from 36 to 22 percent, and from New England, the Midwest, the Southwest, and the West came sizable increases.[70] Between 1987 and 1992, the male enrollment of entering college students decreased from 51 percent to 43 percent, while female enrollment increased to 57 percent from 49 percent.[71]

With the growth in the student population of the college, faculty in the college also grew. Laney inherited 210 arts and sciences faculty in 1977. In 1984, there were 236 faculty members, and by 1992 the number had grown to 328.[72] Approximately one-third of this growth was aided by the Woodruff Endowment, which, by the time of Laney's departure, had added thirty-six distinguished faculty to departments and schools throughout the university. With the growth in faculty also came a broadening of the educational institutions from which the faculty received their doctorates, with a large increase in the number of faculty trained at leading West coast institutions, such as Stanford, Berkeley, and UCLA. In 1977, for instance, only one faculty member was from Stanford, and none were from Berkeley or UCLA. By 1992, eleven faculty members were from Stanford, twelve were from Berkeley, and two were from UCLA. The number of Yale Ph.D.'s during the period 1977 to 1992 grew from six to twenty-three.[73] These changes in the breadth of the faculty reflect Emory's openness to and aggressiveness in recruiting faculty from leading graduate programs nationwide, as well as Emory's attractiveness as a place to teach and work.

As a sign of the seriousness with which Laney and his staff took the need to increase federal research dollars, the faculty in the medical school grew from 589 in 1977 to 671 in 1984 and to 883 in 1992. In the third phase of Laney's administration alone, the medical faculty grew by over 30 percent.[74] According to Charles Hatcher, an intentional decision was made in 1987 to hire faculty for the medical school whose primary function would be research and who could secure large grants, especially from the National Institutes of Health. In addition, a school of public health was started in 1990. This school not only attracted more federal support, but it enabled Emory to build on collaborative relationships with the Centers for Disease Control and the American Cancer Society, both of which were adjacent to the Emory campus. Accompanying the growth in faculty and programs, according to Hatcher, was a tripling of research space, with additions to old facilities and the building of new ones, especially the Rollins Research triangle, which included the new School of Public Health, all at a cost of $45 million.[75]

The growth of the medical establishment at Emory during this period echoes Graham and Diamond's contention that research universities with strong medical programs have the best chance of gaining elite status. They write, "Their [medical schools] powerful magnet of funding for research, education, training, construction, and medical practice has pumped lifeblood into universities and their communities, which otherwise would have been hard hit by rising costs and falling revenues."[76]

With the growth of faculty, especially in the college, concerns increased about the dynamic tension between older, teaching faculty, and newer, research-minded, and better known faculty. Faculty worried that the essential values of the institution might change, given this potentially volatile mix. In general, the university is credited with managing the change in faculty cultures well. In an interview for the *Chronicle of Higher Education* in 1989, Elizabeth Fox-Genovese, who had come to Emory three years earlier to head the women's studies program, expressed her belief that the administration, and Dean Minter in particular, had done a good job of keeping Emory from operating with any kind of "pecking order" among the faculty.[77] As Minter said in this same article, "Star faculty members are respected and esteemed, but they are not treated like royalty."[78]

Despite the finesse with which Laney and his team handled and encouraged the growth in faculty, the growth did not occur without pain along the way. Laney and his team inherited weak programs and were challenged either to direct more money their way or to eliminate them. After careful review and thought, Laney and Minter eliminated the geology department and library science program, and Laney and Hatcher eliminated the dental school. None of these decisions was well-received, especially by alumni, but administrators, backed by the internal review reports and the Lamar Report from the Woodruff gift, felt they had no choice. To build geology into a first-rate program, for instance, would have taken more money than the university was willing to put forth, according to Minter. He studied the budgets of small, leading geology programs in the country. The smallest program, which was at Cornell, received several more times the resources than did Emory's. With the growth in dental and library science programs around the Southeast, especially funded by state schools, Laney and others felt Emory could never adequately compete. Once the decisions were made, the administration stood its ground against the complaints, and their judgment prevailed.[79]

While departments were cut, Laney was also committed to strengthening programs, even if it meant purchasing a department outright. One of the most highly publicized and unusual moves in academe in the late 1980s was Emory's purchase of the entire French department from Johns Hopkins University. This department had been "one of the country's most highly regarded, and...helped Emory vault overnight into the front rank of American universities in French literature studies."[80] The purchase included the top three senior members of the department, as well as ten of the eighteen graduate students.

As the faculty grew, Laney and his staff were concerned to maintain the feeling of community that the university could experience when it was smaller, especially to allow faculty a sense of participation in the governance and direction of the institution. The success of the Phi Beta Kappa symposium in 1979 set the stage for Laney to pursue other means for an intellectual and moral community in the university. The Freshman Seminar described earlier was one attempt to create community between faculty and students. However, Laney was committed to identifying other avenues for faculty community. Recognizing the two cultures of teaching and research that were emerging within the faculty, and the negative effect of the movement toward specialization in research on teaching, Laney pursued vigorously the development of the Luce Seminar for faculty.

The Luce Seminar was to be led by a "public intellectual" who engaged selected faculty, relieved of other teaching obligations, in a semester long exploration of philosophical issues, such as the nature of being human, the nature of knowledge, and the nature of nature itself.[81] In these seminars, faculty were encouraged to think beyond their disciplines in ways that it was hoped would enhance the teaching of their discipline.

To lead the Luce Seminar, Laney secured Dr. James Gustafson, a distinguished professor at the University of Chicago. As an ethicist, Gustafson had gained for himself significant international recognition. Three years into the program, forty-two faculty from diverse disciplines had participated. In a letter to Robert Armstrong, president of the Luce Foundation that funded Gustafson's position, Laney wrote:

> ...in my estimation, the Professorship has been a real and constant force in the development of Emory's temperament and character. By encouraging new connections and supporting those that emerge, the Professorship has been at the center of our evolution toward being a university committed to free and open exchange.... The Seminar itself [is] a kind of microcosm of the University without any a priori answers but a common spirit of inquiry which is larger than one's own discipline.[82]

Like the Freshman Seminar, the Luce Professorship and Luce Seminar were intended to model the moral community so at the heart of Laney's vision for Emory. While no data exist as to its effectiveness in achieving this goal, it is the opinion of Laney and others that it was a successful undertaking in continuing the faculty community Laney had created with the Phi Beta Kappa Symposium.[83]

In the spring of 1993, Laney spoke to Emory's Board of Visitors about what had happened during the year. He enumerated a number of accomplishments by faculty and students. Laney was able to note that much of his vision for Emory in the year 2000 had already been achieved. Research funding had reached $99.7 million in the health sciences alone,[84] and the number of Ph.D. graduates at that year's commencement was 110.[85] What seemed to weigh most heavily on his mind and heart, however, was the third important goal for Emory, which was to maintain its church tradition of training people for service in the world. On the success of this goal, he seemed to take the most pride. He offered this observation to the visitors:

> We are created to serve. If we do not care for something larger than ourselves and do it with a sense of heart, then we ourselves shrivel up. Society, the larger good itself, atrophies. The sense of service and the sense of ambition are twin aspects of education that we must take into account. What it means to be an educated person is not only to be a mind and to seek one's own interests but also to realize that as one enlarges the range of interests and serves them, one is fulfilled.... That is what Emory is about, and I have hope for the future because we are going to exercise that kind of trust and confidence that will make this a better world.[86]

There were rumors that when Laney gave this address he was contemplating stepping down from the Emory presidency. His vision for the institution for the most part accomplished, he may have been ready for another challenge and opportunity. As it turned out, soon after this speech Laney was approached by US President William Clinton to become the US Ambassador to South Korea. With his love for that country still very deep, Laney permitted his name to go forward. Over the course of the summer he submitted to an exhaustive CIA investigation of his background and the Senate confirmation hearings that followed. He was approved, and in October of that year resigned from the presidency, satisfied that Emory was now a major national research university.

Analysis

There is no question that Emory became a major research university during Laney's sixteen-year tenure, although it did not take its place among the elite twelve private universities he used as his goal. The huge growth in Emory's faculty and students had enormous implications for the university's budget. Of all the things that Laney did as president, he remembers the budget taking the majority of his time, especially during the planning phase of November through March of each year. The challenge was not just to set the budget but also to manage the expectations of all involved in the process, especially the deans, an experience, perhaps, all academic presidents in all eras have faced.[87] With the Woodruff gift, a perception existed that Emory could do whatever it wanted. Thus, deans and senior administrators proved themselves quite adept at being creative in trying to access the funds. Yet, for the sheer size of the endowment, the earnings were insufficient to do everything that people wanted.[88]

Between 1977 and 1992, the budget underwent a major transformation. Total current fund expenditures increased from $153,075,000 in 1977 to $891,446,000 in 1992. Tuition and fee income during this period increased from $23,553,000 to $138,102,000, this growth aided by the increased enrollment cited earlier and an annual tuition rate that increased from $3,450 in 1977 to $15,600 in 1992. Student aid grew from $6,255,000 to $95,600,000, with 71 percent of all Emory students receiving some form of financial aid in 1992.[89] Student aid as a percentage of tuition grew from 27 percent to 69 percent. The endowment grew from $178,020,000 to $1,761,965,000, with $570,839,000 of this amount belonging to the Woodruff Endowment. Education and General expenditures increased during this time from $71,203,000 to $419,051,000.[90]

The revenue base of the university during these years was greatly helped not just by the 1000 percent growth of the endowment, but by the huge increase in income from student tuition and fees. At least one of Laney's closest advisors noted that the explosion in programs and stature of Emory during the Laney years was made possible as much by the tuition revenue as it was by the endowment revenue.[91] Students were the beneficiaries of this new revenue, with a respectable $26,000 per student spent on the educational program, a figure that grew by 8 percent alone between 1991 and 1992. Among selected private universities against which Emory compared itself, this spending rate equaled Duke (which actually cut its rate from 1991 to 1992), exceeded Notre Dame, Tulane, and Vanderbilt, and was bested by Stanford, Washington, and Yale.[92]

What these numbers tell is that in an era of retrenchment for many research universities, Emory was able to expand and grow with relative ease. In 1992, for instance, according to data supplied by the American Council on Education (ACE), 34 percent of independent institutions reported no change in spending from the previous year, 29 percent reported budget cuts, and 33 percent reported a 5 to 6 percentage increase. Emory recorded an 8.7 percent increase.[93] Based on the fiscal challenges facing institutions, the ACE offered recommendations encouraging independent institutions to refocus their missions, consolidate programs, initiate new programs to attract new students, such as adult learners, and to consider cuts in inflated student services budgets that were not revenue-producing.[94] The Emory story in the midst of this retrenchment-minded climate was unique, as Emory's strong financial position enabled it to grow and strengthen its commitment to liberal arts education in the college and graduate school thanks to a substantial endowment and healthy enrollment, which produced significant tuition revenues.

Curiously, the attitudes of students in 1992, as reported on the CIRP, would suggest that the Freshman Seminar was not as successful as the administrators hoped nor as altruistic as Laney described. While the era of 1977 to 1992 was a time of great social and cultural change everywhere, the prevailing mood among students nationally was a more conservative approach to life that favored the students' self-interest in most matters. For instance, the "Selected Indicators of Change" reported that at Emory:

> From 1977 to 1992 students attending Emory to make more money increased from 52 to 58 percent, and students attending to get away from home increased from 14 to 28 percent.... At Emory and nationally more students in 1984 than in 1992 performed volunteer work, and fewer attended religious services, drank beer, or worked in a political campaign.... [M]ore students nationally than at Emory value accomplishment in the performing arts and developing a philosophy of life.[95]

What these data suggest is an ambiguous picture of the moral leanings of Emory students in 1992. Admittedly the CIRP instrument is not a moral barometer and it is difficult to draw definitive inferences from the data supplied, but in the absence of any other data, it is appropriate to note that for all of Laney's attention to the moral community a sense of moral community was not uniformly manifest in student attitudes in quite the way he might have hoped.

One of the most interesting pieces of data from this era, and one of the great myths perpetuated by Emory administrators of this time,[96] is that Emory was by 1992 the first choice of institution for a larger number of students; in fact, the percentage actually declined from 1977. In 1977, 72 percent of freshman reported Emory as their first choice. By 1992, that number had declined to 65 percent, with 12 percent indicating that Emory was less than their second choice. The national average for students attending the school of their first choice was 75 percent.[97]

Thus, in 1992, Emory was well below the national norm of highly selective private universities. This can be explained in part by the increasing competition for students during this era, coupled with the declining market of students. Yet, other selective private universities faced the same demographic challenges and, for the most part, their percentage of first choice students remained higher.[98] While Emory's stature may have risen nationally, then, it was not great enough to attract a higher percentage of first-choice students, relative to the norm of similar institutions.

Further evidence that more students were coming to Emory likely as a second or third choice after being denied by Midwestern and New England schools is seen in the surprising drop in Southern and Georgia enrollment during the third phase of Laney's administration, a drop that returned the percentages to the 1977 numbers of 47 percent and 19 percent respectively.[99] At the 1987 trustee retreat, Laney and his staff celebrated the achievement of the increasing Southern enrollment at the college, a major issue for Laney when he came into office. As the focus of the vision for the university became more national in scope, it seems that Emory slighted its commitment to its Southern roots and constituency in favor of admitting more students from New England and the Midwest.

That Emory's reputation soared nationally during Laney's tenure is confirmed by a number of external authorities. Howard Lamar, for instance, who authored the Lamar Report was able to offer this observation to the Emory trustees at their 1987 retreat before any of the accomplishments of Laney's third phase were known:

> I can say truthfully that in the country at large academic people are no longer talking about the Woodruff gift at Coca-Cola University. They are talking instead about scholars at Emory, about your graduate program, and about your fantastic scholarships. You're being talked

about as a new Hopkins or a new Chicago, but I know that you plan to be a very different national university. I would say that your message is now going out, and that disinterested persons perceive that this is a place where good scholars are going.[100]

National publications and national organizations took note of Emory's progress in their rankings and ratings. *US News and World Report* in its annual college rankings placed Emory in the top twenty-five nationally ranked universities in 1987, 1988, 1992, and 1993.[101] Emory's Carnegie classification was changed from Research II to Research I within the year that Laney left office. While this change did not occur on Laney's watch, few would deny Laney the rightful claim that the changes he engineered at Emory during his tenure resulted in this change in rating.

The greatest recognition of Emory's increase in prominence was its election in 1994 to the prestigious AAU. Laney had sought membership in this organization from the time of his election to the presidency, and his failure to secure election for Emory during his tenure was a bitter disappointment to him.[102] While Laney had identified as early as 1977 that his goal for Emory was membership in the AAU, the lobbying efforts to make this happen did not intensify until the mid 1980s. This took place at the conclusion of the second phase and the beginning of the third phase of Laney's administration, when it was expected that the AAU membership would be holding elections for new members.

Laney believed that Emory was due membership in the AAU because of his perception that Emory was as accomplished, and, in some cases, more so than some of the current membership. He knew that Emory had been handicapped in its candidacy for membership because of the relative youth of its graduate program. But these concerns did not dissuade

Laney from using every means at his disposal to gain membership in the AAU.

Included in the measures Laney took to gain membership in the AAU was enlisting the aid of President Carter in 1985 in making contact with Donald Kennedy, president of Stanford and a leading voice in AAU matters, about supporting Emory's bid. Laney wrote to Carter: "I know that President Giamatti of Yale is going to speak in our favor, and Derek Bok of Harvard is the president of the AAU this year, and he is a friend. If Donald Kennedy could be persuaded to speak [for us] I think we would stand a very good chance of getting in."[103] Laney also had his provost, Billy Frye, communicate to all the deans in the university about undertaking "low key 'lobbying'" efforts with the presidents of member schools, with a list of member schools and their presidents accompanying the memorandum.[104]

In his 1987 letter of application to Robert Rosenzweig, the director of the AAU, Laney presented Emory's case for membership in the AAU this way: "Our aim is to see Emory recognized among the finest 20 or 25 universities in the nation within the decade…. I believe that Emory's distinctive quality, its importance to this city and region, and its extraordinary dynamism warrant consideration of its admission to this select group."[105] For a third time, Laney's efforts at admission failed, and after 1987, there is never mention again in any of Laney's public statements about seeking membership in the AAU. So strong was his disappointment that he indicated in an interview that had Emory been elected to the AAU while he was still in office toward the end of his tenure, he would have declined the invitation.[106]

Finally, Emory's national prominence was recognized in 1997 by the exhaustive study of national universities conducted by Hugh Graham and Nancy Diamond. In this study, Graham and Diamond demonstrate the fluid hierarchy of national research universities in the post World War II era. They argue that a perception has existed that a closed cadre of elite universities existed prior to and after World War II, and that this perception has been reinforced by flawed reputational surveys that fail to take into account broad institutional data, such as scholarly publications across all disciplines, while also controlling for institutional size. Using their analysis, which accounted for faculty size, student enrollment, scholarly publication record, and research and development funding, Graham and Diamond found that Emory was nineteenth out of twenty-three private universities in the nation. In this group of twenty-three, Emory was only one of three institutions not on the 1987 Carnegie Research I classification. Despite having a Carnegie Research II classification, Graham and Diamond argue that based on 1990 data they used for their study, Emory qualified as a "challenger" institution to those institutions believed to have "elite" status.[107]

Graham and Diamond's study notes one fact that must be considered a weakness of Laney's third phase, the lack of success in bringing on more new faculty. At the 1987 trustee retreat, Minter, in his report on the college, noted that for the college to offer the quality education it desired, and simultaneously improve the research record of the faculty, a faculty contingent of 425 would be essential.[108] In 1984, the faculty number in the college stood only at 236 and by 1992, although the growth was significant, it had only reached 328, nearly 100 shy of Minter's projection. There is no doubt that the inability to increase the size of the college faculty faster, and, thereby, avoid the negative effects this would have on the full development of the graduate program, contributed to Emory's not receiving an invitation to join the AAU before mid-1990. In this respect, the growth of Emory did not keep pace with Laney's ambition.

The Laney years were a time of remarkable growth in virtually every respect for Emory. In the three phases of the Laney administration from 1977 until 1993 the steps for taking Emory from a regional teaching institution to a major national research university are discernible. In each of the phases, initiatives were taken to improve the quality of the liberal arts program by focusing on the college and the graduate school, as had been done at elite private universities, such as Harvard, Johns Hopkins, and Chicago in the late nineteenth century. The number and quality of students and faculty were significantly improved by the developments at Emory. While all the changes did not go as Laney had hoped, such as admission to the AAU, nor as he believed, such as the strong moral development of students and Emory's being a first choice of college for more students, Laney's efforts were rewarded by the increased national recognition the university received prior to and soon after his departure. None of the changes of these sixteen years was without some challenge and difficulty along the way from a variety of sources. The next chapter will explore the nature of these difficulties, how Laney addressed them, and how in his handling of them he demonstrated his commitment to moral leadership.

---

[1] James T. Laney, interview by author, tape recording, Emory University, Atlanta, 11 November 1997.

[2] Frederick Rudolph, *The American College and University: A History* (New York: Alfred A. Knopf, Inc., 1983) 336, citing Charles Eliot in Samuel Eliot Morison, *Three Centuries of Harvard, 1636–1936* (Cambridge: Harvard University Press, 1936) 336.

[3] Laurence Veysey, *The Emergence of the American University* (Chicago: University of Chicago Press, 1965) 376.

[4] Rudolph, *The American College and University*, 343.

[5] See chapter 2 for a detailed review of Laney's position on the liberal arts and moral community.

[6] Billy E. Frye, *A Vision for Emory: A Report from the Chancellor* (Atlanta: Emory University, 1998) 2–3.

[7] Henry M. Bullock, *A History of Emory University* (Nashville: Parthenon Press, 1936) 346–60.

[8] Frye, *A Vision for Emory*, 2.

[9] David R. Levine, *The American College and the Culture of Aspiration, 1915–1940* (Ithaca NY: Cornell University Press, 1986) 78–82.

[10]Bullock, *A History of Emory University*, 320–60.

[11]Frye, *A Vision for Emory University*, 2. See discussion in chapters 1 and 3 about some of the disappointments of the Martin and Atwood presidencies of this era.

[12]Frye, *A Vision for Emory University*, 2.

[13]The professional schools were business, medicine, nursing, theology, law, and dentistry. The divisions were allied health professions and library science. Although Emory College was officially moved from Oxford to Atlanta in 1919, the university retained the Oxford campus. Its uses have varied over the years, but since 1929 it has functioned as a junior college, providing a steady stream of transfer students to Emory in Atlanta their junior and senior years.

[14]Susan H. Frost, "Emory University 1977, 1984, 1992 (Academic Year): Selected Indicators of Change," February 1994, Office of Institutional Planning and Research, Emory University, Atlanta, document not numbered (hereafter, "Selected Indicators of Change"). My access to demographic, statistical, and financial data was limited to this comprehensive, and very helpful, report. Thus, comparisons I will make will be limited to the data from this report, which includes the years 1977, 1984, and 1992.

[15]Frost, "Selected Indicators of Change."

[16]Laney interview, 11 November 1997.

[17]William H. Fox, interview by author, note recording, Emory University, Atlanta, 7 July 1998; copyrighted notes by J. Thomas Bertrand on "Leadership of James T. Laney at Emory University," in author's possession, July 1997.

[18]Elizabeth Coe, "Laney Announces Fund Drive," *The Wheel* 61/3 (11 October 1979): 9.

[19]Laney interview, 11 November 1997.

[20]Laney interview, 11 November 1997.

[21]Gary S. Hauk, *A Legacy of Heart and Mind: Emory Since 1836* (Atlanta: Emory University, 1999) 145.

[22]"General Faculty Meeting," 1 February 1978, Laney Papers, box 21, folder "Faculty," RWWL, 1–2.

[23]"General Faculty Meeting," 1 February 1978, Laney Papers, 3–5.

[24]"General Faculty Meeting," 1 February 1978, Laney Papers, 6.

[25]Charles T. Lester to members of the Advisory Committee for the Evaluation of Emory's Capital Needs, 26 February 1979, Laney Papers, box 4, folder "Capital Needs Committee Report," RWWL, 1–8.

[26]See chapter 3 for a description of the role that Robert and George Woodruff played in the success of the campaign, as well as how Laney—in this first phase of

his administration—took great care to cultivate the interest and support of Robert Woodruff for the direction Emory was moving.

[27]Dr. Charles Hatcher, Jr., interview by author, note recording, Emory University, Atlanta, 14 July 1998. Dr. Hatcher was director of the Emory Clinic at the time of this negotiation. In 1983, he was elevated to the position of Vice President for Health Affairs. In this interview, Hatcher noted with humor that he had predicted the 10 percent requirement before Laney even proposed it, figuring that a clergyman—which Laney was—would want a "tithe" on the earnings.

[28]Emory was not unique in having this opinion of its medical establishment. As Graham and Diamond note, nearly all research universities with medical schools face similar challenges. They write, "Medical schools, jealous of their fiscal and administrative autonomy, have not been convenient cash cows for their parent universities...." See Hugh Graham and Nancy Diamond, *The Rise of American Research Universities: Elites and Challengers in the Postwar Era* (Baltimore: Johns Hopkins University Press, 1997) 210.

It should be noted that in phase three Laney renegotiated the clinic's contribution to the university, with an even larger percentage of its earnings coming to the University. According to Hatcher, the move was highly controversial.

[29]Laney interview, 11 November 1997.

[30]"Symposium Announcement," no date, Laney Papers, box 21, folder "Faculty," RWWL, 1.

[31]"Preface to the Issue: Intellect and Imagination," *Daedalus: Journal of the American Academy of Arts and Sciences* 109/2 (Spring 1980) viii.

[32]"Preface to the Issue: Intellect and Imagination," viii. Stanley Cavell and Judith Shklar both became members two years later of the Lamar Committee that reviewed Emory and its opportunities with the Woodruff gift.

[33]Laney interview, 11 November 1997.

[34]"Report to Faculty," 2 December 1982, Laney Papers, box 25-2, folder "Speaking Engagements 1985–1986 [sic]," RWWL, 1.

[35]"Report to Faculty," Laney Papers, 2.

[36]"Report to Faculty," Laney Papers, 3.

[37]"Report to Faculty," Laney Papers, 4.

[38]David Minter, telephone conversation with author, LaGrange GA, 7 July 1998.

[39]Minter interview.

[40]"Transcription of Remarks Presented at the Trustee Retreat," 13-14 March 1987, Laney Papers, box 10, folder "Trustees Retreat 1987," RWWL, 42.

[41]Frost, "Selected Indicators of Change," see "Emory University Enrollment, 1977–1992."

[42]In this second phase of Laney's administration, it is impossible to quantify the qualitative improvement in students, as Emory only began collecting data on average SAT scores and average GPAs in 1984. Virtually all administrators believe there was improvement, given that the Woodruff Fellowships began being awarded in 1981.

[43]James T. Laney, "Annual Meeting of Board of Visitors," 23 April 1986, Laney Papers, box 25-1, pocket 3, RWWL, 4.

[44]Much of the momentum for change in student life occurred in the first phase of Laney's administration. However, it was not until 1981 that Laney would permanently name William Fox to the post of vice president for campus life. Thus, all of the initiatives Dr. Fox undertook occurred in the second and third phases of Laney's administration.

[45]The UAA is an NCAA Division III—non-scholarship—conference and includes the following major independent research universities: Brandeis, Carnegie-Mellon, Case-Western Reserve, Emory, Johns Hopkins, New York, Chicago, Rochester, and Washington. In 1990, Laney wrote with pride that this athletic association proved that "good athletes who are also high academic achievers can compete well, can stimulate interest, and can balance athletics and academics" (James T. Laney, "Through Thick and Thin: Two Ways of Talking about the Academy and Moral Responsibility," in *Ethics in Higher Education*, ed. William W. May [New York: American Council on Education, 1990] 65).

[46]William H. Fox, interview by author, 7 July 1998, note recording, Emory University, Atlanta.

[47]"Trustee Retreat," Laney Papers, 9.

[48]Minter interview.

[49]James T. Laney, "The Moral Authority of the President," April 1983, *Heart*, 9. See also Laney, "Through Thick and Thin," 63.

[50]Fox and Minter interviews.

[51]"Trustee Retreat," Laney Papers, 43.

[52]"Trustee Retreat," Laney Papers, 47.

[53]"Trustee Retreat," Laney Papers, 44.

[54]"Trustee Retreat," Laney Papers, 44.

[55]"Announcement by President James T. Laney At Monday or Tuesday Press Conference," no date, box 23-2, "Correspondence Notebook April–June 1986 [sic]," RWWL, 2.

[56]"Celebrity Professors: Do They Pay Off for Colleges and Students?," *Newsweek on Campus* (September 1987): 9.

[57]*Heart*, vii.

[58]Laney, "Annual Meeting of Board of Visitors," Laney Papers, 3.

[59]Laney, "Annual Meeting of Board of Visitors," Laney Papers, 2.

[60]This bequest was in addition to the $105 million he and his brother, Robert, gave Emory in 1979.

[61]Billy E. Frye to James T. Laney, 4 February 1987, box 5, folder "Graduate School," RWWL, 2.

[62]"Trustee Retreat," Laney Papers, 10. In the transcription of Laney's remarks, the twelve schools are not listed, but based on his remarks I would judge that the schools were these: Harvard, Yale, Stanford, Chicago, Johns Hopkins, Pennsylvania, Brown, MIT, Cornell, Columbia, Princeton, and Dartmouth. It is curious to note that Laney does not acknowledge the strength of Duke and Vanderbilt as "aspiring" institutions. Later it will be shown that Duke and Vanderbilt both emerge as leading private universities in the 1980s and early 1990s. While Emory seems to be slightly below Vanderbilt in most of the rankings cited by Graham and Diamond, Duke is most often rated in the top ten nationally (Graham and Diamond, *The Rise of American Research Universities*, 177, 183, 185, 186, 188, 197).

At the trustee retreat, Laney offered these observations about Vanderbilt and Duke, "...I would say that Emory's distinction from Vanderbilt and Duke lies in this. Vanderbilt has largely left behind its concern for values, as it has become gentrified. Its cultural cachet is that it is the place for southern gentry and that's a very attractive thing.... I think that puts a ceiling that is unfortunate upon the aspirations of the university. I think that Duke is unashamedly and unabashedly seeking to be like the Ivy League. Now that's my distinction between Duke and Vanderbilt. Emory's distinctive role—and it is one we have not yet fully claimed—is to unite value and merit in a way that enhances the true growth of the whole person" ("Trustee Retreat," Laney Papers, 15).

[63]"Trustee Retreat," Laney Papers, 53.

[64]"Trustee Retreat," Laney Papers, 13.

[65]"Trustee Retreat," Laney Papers, 56.

[66]"Trustee Retreat," Laney Papers, 16.

[67]James T. Laney to Robert Strickland, 3 May 1989, Laney Papers, box 6-8, pt. 1, "Correspondence Notebook May–June 1989," RWWL, 3.

[68]Frost, "Selected Indicators of Change," see "Emory University Enrollment, 1977–1992." Much of the data reported from this point forward will compare fall 1977 figures—the first year of Laney's presidency—to fall 1992 figures—Laney's last full year in office. Laney departed Emory in October 1993.

[69]Frost, "Selected Indicators of Change," see "Emory University: Admission by School, 1977–1992."

[70]Frost, "Selected Indicators of Change," see "Changing Circumstances and Views of Freshmen: Emory and Highly Selective Private Universities." A highly

selective private university was one enrolling a freshman entering class with average SAT scores above 1200.

[71]Frost, "Selected Indicators of Change," see "Emory College: Characteristics of Entering Student."

[72]Frost, "Selected Indicators of Change," see "Emory University: Regular, Full-time Faculty Headcount, 1977–1992 (Academic Years)."

[73]These numbers were tabulated by reviewing the listing of college faculty appointments in the *Emory College Catalogues* for 1977–1978 and 1992–1993.

[74]Frost, "Selected Indicators of Change," see "Emory University: Regular, Full-time Faculty Headcount, 1977–1992 (Academic Years)."

[75]Charles Hatcher, interview by author, 14 July 1998, note recording, Emory University, Atlanta.

[76]Graham and Diamond, *The Rise of American Research Universities*, 210.

[77]Liz McMillen, "Transformation of Emory: A Small Atlanta Institution Is Using a Historic Gift to Vault Into Big-Time Ranks," *Chronicle of Higher Education* 26/4 (27 September 1989): A37.

[78]McMillen, "Transformation of Emory," A37.

[79]Minter interview.

[80]Don Wycliff, "Emory Raises Its Status," *New York Times,* 23 August 1990, A18.

[81]Laney, "Through Thick and Thin," 63.

[82]James T. Laney to Robert E. Armstrong, 30 March 1992, Laney Papers, box 6-8, pt. 5, "Correspondence Notebook, March–July 1992," RWWL.

[83]Frye, Laney, and Minter interviews.

[84]Frost, "Selected Indicators of Change," see "The Woodruff Health Sciences Center: Sponsored Research FY88-FY93."

[85]Frost, "Selected Indicators of Change," see "Emory University: Degrees Granted by School, 1977–1992."

[86]James T. Laney, "Board of Visitors," 12 May 1993, Laney Papers, box 25-1, pocket 7, RWWL, 7, 11.

[87]Richard Storr, *Harper's University: The Beginning* (Chicago: University of Chicago Press, 1966) 241. Storr says that Harper found the budget and managing expectations at Chicago a "'duty more onerous than any other.'" According to Storr, Harper once presented the challenge to the trustees in this way, "'My work consists very largely in denying requests for additional money and in opposing plans which require for their execution the expenditure of money.'"

[88]Laney interview, 11 November 1997.

[89]This figure was not kept in 1977.

[90]Frost, "Selected Indicators of Change," see "Emory University: Financial Highlights, 1977–78 to 1992–93."

[91]Frye interview.

[92]Frost, "Selected Indicators of Change," see "Emory and Selected Private Universities Spending on Educational Program per Student."

[93]Frost, "Selected Indicators of Change," see "Emory Focuses on Excellence as the ACE Recommends that Universities Restructure."

[94]Frost, "Selected Indicators of Change," see "Emory Focuses on Excellence as the ACE Recommends that Universities Restructure."

[95]Frost, "Selected Indicators of Change," see "Changing Circumstances and Views of Freshmen: Emory and Highly Selective Private Universities."

[96]"Myth" is used here intentionally because almost every administrator interviewed had the opinion that Emory was increasingly the place students wanted to come to. With the more diverse student population Emory attracted and the improvement of the quality of the students enrolled, this perception is understandable. However, the data suggest that although Emory students may have been more diverse and brighter, Emory was not for 35 percent of them their first choice.

[97]Frost, "Selected Indicators of Change," see "Changing Circumstances and Views of Freshman: Emory and Highly Selective Private Universities."

[98]Frost, "Selected Indicators of Change," see "Changing Circumstances and Views of Freshman: Emory and Highly Selective Private Universities."

[99]Frost, "Selected Indicators of Change," see "Emory College: Characteristics of Entering Students."

[100]"Trustee Retreat," Laney Papers, 72. For more information on the Lamar Report, the reader is referred to chapter 3 and the discussion of the external report prepared for Emory's use after the Woodruff gift was made.

[101]See the 26 October 1987, 10 October 1988, 28 September 1992, and 4 October 1993 issues of *US News and World Report*.

[102]James T. Laney to George Rupp, 16 August 1985, Laney Papers, box, 9, folder "Rice University Inauguration," RWWL. Rupp was the newly elected president of Rice at the time of this letter. Laney's letter includes the following, "I also wanted to say how delighted I am that Rice has been admitted into the AAU. Your good fortune compensates for my own disappointment that Emory was passed over….But there will be another opportunity the next go round, and we will continue to press for Emory's 'rightful' place in that association."

[103]James T. Laney to Jimmy Carter, 27 February 1985, Laney Papers, box 2, folder "AAU," RWWL.

[104]Billy E. Frye to colleagues (academic deans), 6 April 1987, Laney Papers, box 5, folder "Graduate School," RWWL.

[105]James T. Laney to Robert Rosenzweig, 15 May 1987, Laney Papers, box 5, folder "Graduate School," RWWL.

[106]Laney interview, 11 November 1997.

[107]Graham and Diamond, *The Rise of American Research Universities,* 176–78. It should be noted that Graham and Diamond consider Emory one of eleven private universities to have made significant strides during the 1980s. On the list of eleven, Graham and Diamond place Emory ninth in its transformation. Their list includes the following institutions in the order presented: Brandeis, Rochester, Washington, Carnegie Mellon, Vanderbilt, Notre Dame, Rice, Dartmouth, Emory, Tufts, and Tulane (p. 196).

[108]"Trustee Report," Laney Papers, 48.

CHAPTER FIVE

LANEY AS MORAL LEADER
Challenges to the Laney Presidency

It is often said by those who study leadership that the sign of a mature and effective leader is the way she/he handles challenge and crisis.[1] In this regard, the Laney presidency makes a very good case study, as in his sixteen year tenure there were challenges and crises that could have thwarted his aspirations for Emory's transformation and seriously jeopardized his presidency. While at times Laney's handling of crisis moments lacked uniformity and evenness, his approach demonstrated his deep commitment to the moral community he wanted at Emory and to the academic president being a moral leader.

Among academic presidents, Laney was not alone in having challenge and crisis in his administration, as a presidency of any significant duration is bound to have unhappy times of trial and difficulty. This was certainly true for Eliot, who, in his forty-year tenure at Harvard, was criticized by Protestant churches for the open acceptance that he demonstrated to Catholics, in an era and a region of the country where anti-Catholic sentiment was strong. Simply by permitting Catholic speakers for lectures or Catholic priests for worship services, Eliot was branded as "papalizing."[2] Harper was continually dogged with financial concerns for the institution that he helped birth, with worry that negative publicity or misunderstanding about actions taken by the institution could have a deleterious effect financially.[3]

In the age of the Red Scare, Hutchins faced charges in 1935 by Walgreen that Chicago was using "subversive materials.... [with]

'Communist influences'" in some of its classes. The charge became a rallying cry for conservative-minded citizens, and, eventually Hutchins found himself defending the university before an Illinois senate committee, which was investigating the matter.[4] Bond had challenges of his own at Lincoln with alumni unhappy about the state of the athletic program, with legatees who were denied admission because of poor academic backgrounds, with sectarian conservatives troubled by his "religious liberalism," and with trustees and funders over his failure to implement the New Plan, which called for an attempt to attract a larger percentage of white students to the institution.[5]

How presidents address the challenges of their administrations depends upon the dynamics of the era and the issues, and their own personalities, as the experiences of Eliot, Harper, Hutchins, and Bond indicate. Eliot and Harper were spared any significant loss of authority and power through their deft handling of their challenges, although the emotional strain of the financial concerns at Chicago might well have led to Harper's untimely death while in office at forty-nine years of age. The investigation that confronted Hutchins and Chicago resulted in a loss of confidence for Hutchins by the trustees, a negative opinion of the university, and a drop in student enrollment and gift income, according to Dzuback. Yet, Hutchins' vigorous and articulate defense of the university against outside influence was among his most enduring legacies, and this enabled him to persevere at Chicago for another sixteen years, despite ongoing conflicts with the faculty.[6] Bond was unable to overcome the turmoil of his tenure at Lincoln, resulting, finally, in his dismissal from office in 1957.[7] The dynamics of Laney's era, his own personality, and his commitment to the moral dimensions of academic leadership determined the outcome of the issues with which he was confronted during his administration.

Challenges by the Church

As Laney's tenure as president grew longer and as the accomplishments of the United Methodist-related Emory became more nationally visible, Laney was often called on to deliver speeches at national church gatherings and at other United Methodist-related colleges, such as DePauw and Wofford. By the accounts of many who worked in the national church hierarchy, he was regarded as the quintessential clergyman-president—visionary, well-read, articulate, and passionate on moral issues and moral development of students. What Laney achieved at Emory was a source of pride for the national church, as evidenced by his invitation in 1992 to speak to the 400-person gathering of the Board of Higher Education and Ministry at the quadrennial general confernece of the United Methodist Church,[8] and later that year as a keynote speaker for the quintennial meeting of the World Methodist Council.[9]

Curiously, over the time of Laney's tenure at Emory, his standing with many local United Methodists, especially those in North Georgia, diminished. While the opinion was not universally shared, an erosion of support for his leadership occurred locally, namely over issues that were controversial to the church at the time, such as the consumption of alcohol, the selling of pornography on campus, the establishment of an office for gays/lesbians/bisexuals, and the inclusion of sexual orientation in the school's Equal Opportunity Statement. His challenge to the bishop and cabinet[10] of the North Georgia Conference over the pastoral leadership serving the Glenn Memorial United Methodist Church, located on the campus, also contributed to a diminution of support. That his support eroded over time can be seen by the fact that he failed to win reelection by his clergy peers from the North Georgia Conference for a delegate spot to the General and Jurisdictional conferences after 1979.[11] Many of his peers were not satisfied with his defense of the university over some of the practices they found objectionable.

The first difficult church-related issue Laney faced was in 1979 over the attempt of the university to sell alcohol on campus. Laney had supported a recommendation from a trustee committee on student life urging that a separate corporation be established to apply for a license for the sale of beer and wine, along with food, in a site adjacent to campus. The school newspaper wrote a story about this initiative that contained a number of misrepresentations, according to Laney, one of which was that he was "cavalier in [his] attitude toward County authority and callous with regard to the long-standing Methodist concern about drinking."[12]

The story from the school newspaper was carried in the Atlanta newspaper[13] and a denominationally-owned paper. Reactions to the story were highly negative, and Laney received many disapproving letters.[14] To quell the public opinion over the incident, Laney deemed it prudent to write a letter to all clergy of the North Georgia Conference stating his position. His letter, addressed to "Dear Colleagues in Ministry," offered as a defense that many United Methodists no longer abide by the church's teaching about the non-consumption of alcohol and that Emory was simply trying to deal responsibly with a reflection of the times. He noted, too, that the strength of the church-relatedness of the university should be determined more by the witness of the institution than by taboos. He explained about the numerous initiatives the university had undertaken since his arrival that spoke to the importance of the church relationship, such as the hiring of a new chaplain and a new campus minister, the latter in cooperation with the Glenn Memorial United Methodist Church. Laney concluded his two page memorandum:

> The construction of the Cannon Chapel, the strengthening of our Christian Ministry on campus, and the clear identification I have with the Methodist Church would seem to establish, in many ways, for the first time in more than a quarter of a century a basis for warm and

cordial relations between the Church and the University…. For your information, when my wife and I moved into Lullwater [the president's home] we made a conscious decision not to serve alcohol on social occasions. This we feel is the more appropriate kind of fidelity to tradition which you expect of me. Not every action that I take will meet with your approval, I am sure. But I do hope that the direction of the University as a whole in the months and years ahead, will, nevertheless, warrant your confidence.[15]

An especially public embarrassment for the university regarding alcohol on campus was the photograph that ran in the *Atlanta Journal and Constitution* following the 1989 commencement ceremony that showed students consuming champagne. The writer who covered the ceremony, which featured US Senator Sam Nunn as the speaker, described the audience as filled with "thousands of champagne-guzzling soon-to-be graduates" and that the ceremony was punctuated with "the sound of champagne corks popping in the audience."[16] Numerous letters came to Laney expressing surprise and disappointment at the way students comported themselves.[17] One characteristic letter signed "a disappointed graduate" from the class of 1931 with copies sent to "several bishops," concluded: "Emory had disgraced herself and her older graduates are hanging their heads in shame. The Methodist Church should come out with a strong denunciation or it too will lose face."[18] In reply, Laney wrote that the newspaper article was misleading and that only a handful of students had behaved inappropriately. Laney promised that a review of the ceremony had been conducted and that steps would be taken to ensure that such unruliness would not occur in the future. Yet, in the end, Laney could not but help agree with the complaining graduate. Laney's candor no doubt surprised him when he wrote: "As unhappy as I

am with the newspaper account, I am even more unhappy with the conduct of that small group of undergraduates. They not only disgraced
themselves and disappointed their parents and families, but they have
given a bad name to their classmates and to the entire University."[19] Such
was the directness and honesty that Laney used in his dealings with those
who would be critical of him or the university.

In addition to the sale of alcohol on campus, Laney also received criticism about the sale of *Playboy* and *Playgirl* in the university bookstore.
The objection was widespread, but came mostly from persons who
attended the university's Course of Study program, which trained sec-
ond-career persons for the ministry without their having to earn a
master's degree. Typically, the students were from rural areas, where
church opinion on these issues was much more conservative. In addition
to letters from the students themselves, Laney received letters from members of these students' churches and from their bishops to whom the
students had complained.[20]

In response to the criticism Laney received about the sale of *Playboy*
and *Playgirl*, he noted that the university's practice was not that unusual
and in keeping with peer church-related institutions, such as Duke and
SMU, which sold this literature. Furthermore, he argued that a distinction had to be made between church-related and the church. As a
church-related university, Laney argued that Emory had no choice but to
sell this literature out of respect for the time-honored tradition of academic freedom central to the purpose of higher education. He explained
himself to a bishop in this manner:

> ...while I am not interested in supporting *Playboy* as
> wholesome reading matter, I am interested in a
> University as a bastion of free speech, the bedrock upon
> which all universities must rest.... The University must
> guard against having any kind of intrusion from out-

> side…. The very point of a university community is
> open discussion and decision freely arrived at. One of the
> most delicate and difficult things that I have to do is to
> assist some pastors…to understand that the University,
> although connected to the Church, is *not* the Church.
> That is to say, we cannot impose the standards of the
> Church upon a pluralistic University community, but
> have to bring the influence to bear in a more subtle and
> educative fashion. This may not be satisfactory to many
> people. But it is consistent with the integrity of a com-
> munity of intellectual inquiry.[21]

Laney used this same logic in supporting the inclusion of sexual orientation in the university's Equal Opportunity Statement in 1993. For Laney,
it was a matter of justice that gays and lesbians be included in the statement, despite church positions that viewed homosexuality as
incompatible with Christian teaching.[22]

Along with Emory's failure to achieve admission to the AAU during
Laney's tenure, there was no greater personal disappointment of his
administration than his failure to heighten the prominence of the role
and pastoral leadership of the Glenn Memorial United Church. Glenn
Memorial was built on the Emory campus in 1931 through generous
gifts from Mr. and Mrs. Charles Howard Candler, Thomas K. Glenn,
and others to memorialize the five decades of service to the North
Georgia Conference by the Reverend Wilbur Fisk Glenn (1839–1922),
who graduated from Emory College in 1861.[23] The intent of the church
was to have a dual function as a worshipping congregation of the North
Georgia Conference and to serve as an auditorium for the university
where convocations, lectures, concerts, and recitals might be held.

The dual functionality of Glenn Memorial continues to this day, but
Laney believed he had a unique opportunity to make Glenn Memorial

more than just a church of the North Georgia Conference. With the Duke University Chapel as his model, he wanted Glenn Memorial to be served by a pastoral leader who had a national profile and could teach in Emory's religion department or the Candler School of Theology. It seemed only natural to Laney that his ordained status and the progress of the university were the necessary ingredients to create of the Glenn Memorial Church something innovative and exciting in higher education and for the national church. To Laney's dismay his view of the unique opportunity was never shared by the bishop or the cabinet.

Laney began his lobbying efforts for Glenn Memorial soon after his election as president, first privately with the bishop and select members of the clergy. Frustrated that these efforts proved fruitless, Laney elected in 1988 to appoint a high powered task force of Glenn Memorial Church members, Emory administrators, and clergy from outside the conference to conduct a study on the possibilities for a strengthened and expanded relationship between Emory and Glenn Memorial. The cost of the study was $23,000.[24]

After months of review, the report reached this conclusion about the need for strengthened pastoral leadership at Glenn Memorial:

> While Glenn has been intentional about its community ministry, it has done less to strengthen its witness either as a leading church in the wider Atlanta community or as a vital Christian presence on the Emory campus. Glenn must meet the challenge of developing into a "public church," offering its members a strong worship and educational experience *and* finding ways for the congregation to serve the city and the campus. Much of the task of strengthening Glenn Memorial must be led by strong pastors, who give active and creative witness both in the pulpit and in the program outreach of the church.

> Ways must be found to work with the United Methodist officials to bring pastors of unusual talent and grace as ministers of Glenn. At the same time the Glenn congregation must be stimulated and inspired to envision the unusual opportunities offered to the church.[25]

Laney sent this report to each of the active bishops of the Southeastern Jurisdiction, several of whom were members of the Emory board of trustees. The files suggest that none of the bishops, including the bishop of the North Georgia Conference, wrote a reply, even acknowledging receipt of the report. Though not distributed to the clergy of the North Georgia Conference, the report's conclusions were widely known to many in the area. Many clergy, especially, became frustrated with Laney for exercising what they perceived as heavy-handedness in trying to determine the pastoral appointment of one of the conference's leading churches.

One bishop outside of the jurisdiction to whom the report was sent, and whose son at one time Laney privately hoped would be appointed to serve Glenn Memorial, did send a reply. He no doubt summarized well Laney's own frustration with what Laney came to believe was the parochial vision of the leadership of the North Georgia Conference when he wrote:

> ...the Glenn Church issue strikes at the root of the open wound of our denomination. Appointments are made to benefit clergy. There is no grand strategy for building up the people of God. Not only in this situation, but generally, a church like Glenn is a "plum" appointment to be given to a favorite son [sic] without considering the needs of the congregation. In the Southeast, particularly,

you are up against a bureaucratic authoritarianism designed to serve the clergy first.[26]

Finally recognizing that his hopes for Glenn Memorial would never come to pass, Laney gave up his efforts after this report, never to pursue the matter again, and leaving him greatly discontented.

The accumulation of these church-related issues, which were best known to local Methodists, resulted in a loss of respect for Laney by more conservative-minded church goers. Yet, the opposition to Laney's positions was never so great—thanks, in part, to the forthright manner in which Laney dealt with many of the issues—that the impact on the university from a public relations and fundraising perspective was insignificant. Of course, many church people appreciated the courageousness and progressiveness of Laney's positions. As one of Laney's senior staff noted, "In the same way it took a Nixon to open up China, it took a Laney with his clergyman status to have the 'elbow room' to expand the horizons and liberalize the University's church relationship."[27] A non-clergy president might not have had the same effectiveness in dealing with these issues as did Laney.

The Great Park Debate

Aside from concerns about alcohol on campus and frustrations from people in the church, one of Laney's greatest challenges came internally from his own faculty who opposed with vehemence the building of the Presidential Parkway, which would provide access to the Carter Presidential Library and Conference Center. The opposition made Laney very vulnerable, as he had been integral to the recruitment of Carter to Atlanta and to his professorship in the university. Moreover, Laney had an understanding with Carter that eventually the university would take over management of the center at the time of Carter's retirement. Carter was adamant that the use of the center was dependent upon easy access to it, which required the building of a four lane access road through a residential neighborhood adjacent to Emory, continuing to the interstate. Laney's files document the numerous letters of complaint he received from community leaders and faculty, urging the university's opposition to the plan. Even trustees were asked to make a public statement about the matter. The files also include a three-page diary that describes the development of the issue over the thirteen years it was debated.[28]

As early as 1982, Laney sent a memorandum addressed "To The Emory Faculty," in which he outlined the nature of the dilemma. While indicating his support for the preservation of the neighborhood adjacent to Emory, he noted "the long-term health of the University is also tied to the optimum development of the Great Park, not simply as an extension of our campus, but as an attractive, intrinsically healthy area."[29] He urged continued dialogue on the matter so that all options could be considered.

While the Great Park issue was held in abeyance for several years, it intensified in importance in 1985, when Professor Dan Carter proposed a resolution "in an extraordinary general meeting [of the faculty]" that expressed the faculty's "resolute opposition to the construction of the proposed 'Presidential Parkway.'" The resolution charged that there had been mishandling of the issue by "improper and unlawful means" and that the project "would degrade the natural and social environment within which [the] university has grown and flourished."[30] A vote on the resolution passed with 461 faculty voting in favor of it, and 144 voting against it.[31] The results of the vote were widely carried in the local press.

The files do not indicate that Laney gave any response to the resolution. Perhaps as a way of protecting Laney, the board chairman, Robert Strickland, issued a university-wide memorandum later that month in which he expressed appreciation for the concerns about the parkway and pointed out that the board's primary interest in the matter had been "to insure an academic environment compatible with the University." He concluded by saying that the trustees would not take a position, offering this defense:

> We see our responsibility as setting and reviewing broad policy to assure the academic and fiscal responsibility of the institution. Beyond these parameters, the Trustees as a body believe it unwise to take positions which might in any way compromise the expression of diverse viewpoints by members of the University community: faculty, staff, students, and alumni.[32]

Laney's silence at this time and the carefully worded statement from Strickland speak to the awkwardness that university officials felt over this matter, given the close relationship many of them enjoyed with Jimmy Carter.[33] Because of pressure from several community groups the matter was eventually resolved without having to involve Laney or the trustees in a public way that would challenge Jimmy Carter. Although many of them may have worked behind the scenes to effect the compromise, which consisted of a shorter, two-lane road through the neighborhood, the files are silent on this point.

South Africa and Apartheid

Simultaneous to the Great Park debate was an issue that confronted many universities in the mid-1980s, which was institutional investments in companies doing business in South Africa. As a moral issue, Laney felt passionately about the improprieties of the practice of apartheid. Laney had traveled previously to that part of the world and had become friends with Archbishop Desmund Tutu, who later in the decade would come to Emory as commencement speaker, receive an honorary degree, and spend a sabbatical. Laney's missionary heart, sensitized by his experiences in

South Korea, caused him to want to be prophetic on this matter. However, to adopt the accepted Sullivan Principles,[34] which encouraged divestment of institutional portfolios of companies doing business in South Africa which did not adhere to the principles, created two major conflicts for him. First, the Emory endowment, by then in excess of $500 million, was principally in Coca-Cola stock, a company whose business presence in South Africa was considerable. This problem was compounded, secondly, by Laney being a member of the Coca-Cola board of directors. Laney, then, was faced with the very difficult task of following the dictates of his heart on the apartheid issue over against the dictates of his loyalty to Emory and Coca-Cola. As it turned out, the matter never went anywhere, and South Africa eventually gained its freedom. However, Laney was still compelled to attempt the part of a prophet on this matter, to some modest success.

At the beginning of the academic year 1985, Laney determined that an Emory-wide, cross-constituent conversation about apartheid was necessary. He named an advisory committee on South Africa, inviting the committee "to sort through the issues presented by the crisis in South Africa and to make recommendations about what we can and should do about them as an academic community."[35] He proposed that among the recommendations the committee might make would be bringing in outside speakers to educate the community on the issue, entering into a faculty and student exchange with universities in that part of the world, and strengthening ties to the South African Church. Laney prefaced his invitation with this impassioned statement reflecting his missionary commitment to the concern:

> Perhaps nowhere in the world today are we faced with a clearer example of the poisonous harvest reaped from policies of racial intolerance than in the Union of South Africa. As we watch the onrushing pace of events there,

it may seem that there is little we can do individually to bring about greater justice and human understanding before even greater tragedy befalls that land. Yet many at Emory feel compelled to do something—not because we aren't also concerned with flagrant abuses of human rights and liberties in other parts of the world, but because as Americans we carry in ourselves a deep sensitivity to the kind of starkly racial injustice so clearly evident in South Africa today.[36]

The files are inconclusive about the recommendations of the final report, but in public presentations about the work of the committee, he noted that two recommendations were especially important to the university. One recommendation was to establish an exchange program for faculty and students with universities in South Africa. A second recommendation was that the investment committee of the board give serious consideration to divestment of stock of those companies continuing to do business in South Africa which had not also signed the Sullivan Principles.[37]

Laney seemed satisfied with the work of the group. He expressed pleasure at the university-wide conversation the issue engendered, as well as the connectedness the Emory community felt to the global community. In one of his articles on this subject he wrote, "The important intangible results lay in the strengthening of bonds among people who were able to step out of their usual roles and see the life of the whole university in terms of global community."[38]

Laney walked a very fine line in dealing with the divestment recommendation. While encouraging the investment committee to study the matter, Laney was challenged to find a means to raise concerns in a non-threatening manner with his colleagues at Coca-Cola. Following a Coca-Cola board meeting in 1986, Laney wrote his views to top company executives Roberto Goizeuta and Donald Keough reminding them that the issue was likely to get more heated in the coming academic year. He presented his case:

> Of course I realize the economic stakes involved and I also know that cogent arguments can be made in behalf of remaining there, both as a company and as general economic policy. I'm not sure however that in the area of image and impression those arguments, however valid, can any longer be heard. We've come to a point in general public opinion that undesired and undesirable connotations will inevitably attach to those corporations which choose to remain there.... I write this with full recognition that my work at Emory will probably be easier if Coca-Cola is not publicly identified with South Africa. But I also think that Coke's life—and fortunes— will prosper more if it is not.[39]

Laney must be credited with dealing with this issue directly with the executives of the company, although it should be noted that he elected to share his thoughts in writing with these gentlemen rather than sharing them in the more public and vulnerable setting of the full board of directors. Whether Goizeuta or Keough responded to this letter, the files do not indicate. The company did sign the Sullivan Principles and it did begin a program of "disinvesting in a way that encouraged black entrepreneurship through a foundation."[40]

In the summer of 1987, the investment committee received a recommendation from its fund manager Trusco about the implications to the university's endowment should the Sullivan Principles be applied. Trusco noted that $22 million of the total endowment was in three companies that operated exclusively in South Africa. Also they stated that employing the Sullivan Principles would remove a significant portion of the larger capitalized companies, including major drug companies, from the portfolio. The minutes of the meeting note that the report was received with appreciation and that no action was taken.[41] By this point, Laney was likely satisfied by the university-wide conversation that had taken place, and he may have been astute enough to know that some trustees were not going to be persuaded by the divestment argument, no matter how morally appropriate to do so. Thus, the issue of divestment was dropped.

Racial Concerns, 1987 and 1990

Of all the issues Laney faced during his presidency none was so painful and difficult nor more likely to threaten his presidency than vehement charges of racism in 1987 and in 1990 that became public spectacles. Laney's handling of both situations demonstrated his skill as a statesman and his passion as clergyman. Of the two incidents the less difficult was the one that occurred in 1987.

During the 1986-1987 academic year several charges of racial insensitivity, especially by Greek organizations, were brought to the attention of the Office of Campus Life by African-American students. Simultaneous with these incidents was the denial of tenure to an African-American, female faculty member, Dr. Sondra O'Neale. She charged that her denial of tenure was evidence of racist practices in the university, and coupled with the other incidents of racial insensitivity, Emory was portrayed in the media as a racist institution.[42] At least one group from outside the university demanded a role in monitoring academic appointments in Emory's Afro-American and African Studies Program.[43]

In response to the allegations of racism, Laney elected to convey his views on the matter to the Emory community through a memorandum addressed "To the Emory Students, Faculty, and Staff." In it, Laney expressed his dismay at the racial incidents and indicated that they would not be tolerated. He reflected on the progress of the university in the last decade to deal with issues of race, such as human relations seminars, and he noted the increase in African-American students and African-American faculty. He, then, tried to separate the tenure case from the racial incidents to show the care and attention used in denying Dr. O'Neale tenure. He noted that she had been given every advantage to meet the research requirement needed to qualify, including two fully paid semesters of leave. He went on to say: "Tenure is a faculty matter. Departments and division-wide faculty committees evaluate recommendations before they are passed on to the President and the Board of Trustees. This is a time-honored process, the protection of which establishes and guarantees the very freedom of the classroom and the integrity of the University which we all cherish."[44] As for the group external to the university wanting a hand in monitoring appointments, Laney responded, "No matter how worthy their professed aims, this kind of external intervention would have the effect of subverting the very integrity and freedom to which this university is unalterably committed."[45] Laney concluded that he pledged his best efforts to ensure that Emory would be a place of justice and equality for all qualified people. This response seemed to satisfy those disaffected in the Emory community for awhile, but undercurrents of tension remained that exploded with fury in 1990.

Following the events in 1987, Laney enlisted the aid of Emory alumnus and Atlanta City Council chairman, Marvin Arrington, in leading a task force to address issues of diversity on campus. The task force determined that an outside study on racial attitudes and conditions at Emory be conducted by Dr. James McClain of Boston. McClain submitted his findings to the Arrington Committee just in advance of the outbreak of racial charges on the campus in 1990.

In late March 1990, a freshman student, Sabrina Collins, alleged that she had received repeated abusive letters, including death threats, from persons she claimed were racist. Over the course of the next week, she contended that she continued to be harassed with racial epithets scrawled on the floor of her dormitory room with fingernail polish, stuffed animals torn, and bleach poured on her clothing. The magnitude of the harassment was such that for a time she became mute. The university responded to her concerns by providing surveillance and other means of support, but her plight became known to others in the Emory community, and individual students and student organizations began to express concern and outrage at what they viewed was a racist institution. For a period of a month, almost daily, the *Atlanta Journal and Constitution* ran stories—many of them on the front page—about the plight of Collins.[46] Eventually, Laney was besieged with phone calls and letters from concerned individuals. Letters of support for Collins, calling for swifter action by the university came from the Student Executive Committee, the College Council, the Student Government Association, the Medical Advisory Council, the Student National Medical Association, the Graduate Business Association, and the Graduate Student Council. Unsolicited offers of assistance came from numerous consultants, eager to secure a job, as well as the Anti-Defamation League of B'nai B'rith, the National Consortium for Black Professional Development, Inc., and the Southern Christian Leadership Conference.[47]

By mid-April there was still no clarity about the identity of the perpetrator, and calls came from several segments of the university to stage protests to force the university to find the person and make the institution more racially sensitive. One letter from "Emory African-American Students" put the challenge this way:

> We the African American students at Emory University are enraged we have been unlawfully and unduly terrorized and discriminated against on the basis of our ethnicity due to a climate which is conducive to and per-

petuates racists [sic] behavior. This pervasive system of racism will no longer be tolerated by the African American community. We would like for Sabrina Collins and her family to know that we support her and pray for her full recovery. In conclusion, we would like to say that this is only the beginning. We now declare Emory University in a state of emergency and if these debilitating conditions persist, we will take further action.[48]

Within days protests were staged, of which Laney attended one but was denied the opportunity to speak, and demands were presented to the administration covering a number of issues.

Just as the protests were picking up, the university began to get word from the Georgia Bureau of Investigation (GBI), which had been studying the case, that it was their conclusion that none of Collins' charges could be substantiated and that Collins had likely inflicted all of the attacks on herself. The rationale for these actions, the GBI speculated, was Collins' poor academic performance in some of her pre-medicine classes that was ending her hope of one day being a doctor.

In this climate, Laney was faced with two difficult challenges. First, he had to find a way to restore order on the campus and faith in the administration. Second, he needed to correct the negative perception of Emory created in Atlanta by the press. And he needed to accomplish both of these objectives without revealing the knowledge that Collins' problems were self-induced.

To address the first challenge of restoring order on campus, Laney issued an open letter to the entire community about the events and held a three-hour meeting with any students who wanted to discuss the matters, without the presence of other administrators. In his letter to the community, Laney thanked members of the community who have "risen up to support Sabrina Collins and her fellow students in their time of distress." While acknowledging the university's continuing cooperation with the GBI, Laney shared with the community that the university would "cover all expenses of Sabrina and those of her family associated with the harassment, an expression of support that [he] reiterated to Sabrina's mother and grandmother when [he] visited with them in Augusta on Sunday morning."[49]

In addition to the letter to the community, Laney also held an open meeting with students the following Sunday evening. In that meeting, Laney made a five-page presentation to the gathering about what he had learned over the previous weeks and what Emory needed to do to address the issues that had been raised. In his presentation, he told the students that he had learned four things from them: that there was not enough of a multi-cultural presence on campus; that not enough had been done to educate the community on racial and gender sensitivity; that tuition was too high and more students need financial help; and that they did not have enough access to him. He continued that he "agreed with [them] in every one of these propositions."[50] Laney proceeded to tell the gathering what Emory was already doing to address these issues, and, in addition, he promised to create a visiting fellows program to be known as the Benjamin Mays Fellows, to establish a multi-cultural center, to offer financial aid packages for entering African-American students that included no loans, and to "personally take charge of this challenge to make Emory a model of multicultural diversity and global awareness."[51] Many of these responses were recommendations that came from the Arrington committee just a few months before.

To counter the challenge of the negative publicity Emory had received in the media, Laney engaged the support of prominent local, African-American alumni and alumnae to sign a letter of support for the University that was published in the *Atlanta Journal and Constitution*. Among those signing the statement were Marvin Arrington, Hamilton Holmes, Michael Lomax, Timothy McDonald, Felker Ward, and Judge

Thelma Wyatt Cummings. In their letter they expressed support for Collins and acknowledged that racial problems existed at Emory, as they did everywhere. They observed: "As much as we hate the disease of racism that caused this pain, however, we object no less to the media hype surrounding it. The media have implied that this incident of harassment is *characteristic* of the racial situation at Emory, and we do not believe that."[52] By having such an outstanding group of African-American citizens express their support for Emory it was hoped that public perception would be somewhat assuaged.

An unanticipated challenge to the openness Laney displayed in handling this matter was the perception by some that he was giving in to demands and was being blackmailed. One of many letters he received from people in the community noted that "the academic standard of the school will take a nose dive as you try to appease the demands of some minorities."[53] Others in the community believed erroneously that Laney agreed to the requiring of an African-American heritage course in the curriculum, prompting one person to write, "why not also Native American, Jewish, Arab, Chinese, Japanese, etc. courses?"[54] Even one faculty member operating under a similar misunderstanding challenged Laney not "to resort to curriculum design by 'crisis management.'"[55] Members of the board were also concerned that Laney might have sold out, as evidenced by a two page memorandum Laney sent to board chairman Strickland, which he, in turn, sent to the other trustees. In this memorandum Laney defended the commitments that he had made as having been "well considered and...part of a longstanding, overall plan and educational philosophy." He concluded forthrightly, "They should be done and they will be done, and they are not being done simply because somebody is making news in the paper."[56] With the school year coming to a close, the community pain Laney had acknowledged began to heal, and the episode quietly came to an end during the summer.

Collins never returned to Emory, and the press eventually revealed the GBI findings in the matter.

Analysis

In these examples of crisis that Laney encountered in his sixteen-year tenure, several recurring themes are worth noting that place him in a long succession of academic presidents who have handled issues similarly. First, the extent to which he would involve himself in the heat of debate and resolution of the issue varied. In the instances of challenges from the church and the racial episodes, Laney demonstrated a central and public role in the handling of these matters. Given his clergyman status, he accepted the responsibility of responding to bishops and others when concerns were expressed about alcohol on campus or the sale of pornography in the bookstore. While his clergyman status did not require that he deal directly with the racial issues, the volatile nature of the episodes and his own convictions about them compelled him to take a front-and-center role in their resolution. Yet, doing so in the case of the racial issues, as we have seen, caused some who were more conservative on race matters to question whether Laney's level of involvement was appropriate.

Laney was less direct in his handling of the Great Park debate. Although initially he addressed the issue, in the heat of the 1985 debate on the matter, he seems to have been virtually silent. Perhaps, for Laney, this was not as significant a moral issue as those of the church and racism, but it cannot be overlooked that he faced enormous political pressure whichever way the issue was resolved. In a similar vein, he did not take as bold a stance as the situation seemed to warrant in the matter of apartheid in South Africa. That this was an issue at all seems to be entirely of Laney's making.[57] He formed the task force to study the matter, and the recommendation about divestment, which he surely knew would be forthcoming, placed him in a considerably awkward situation with Coca-

Cola. The documentary evidence shows that Laney was bold to express his views to the leadership of Coca-Cola; however, he did not encourage divestment when the Trusco report suggested that doing so would have significant implications for the portfolio. His ambivalence on this matter, given his strong statements of support for a moral community committed to the common good at Emory, are surprising in an otherwise impressive record of addressing moral issues. Laney's limited response to these situations could be characterized as the restraint academic presidents felt they needed to exercise for the sake of good institutional health, a phenomenon especially true in the latter twentieth century. Former president Jean Kemeny of Dartmouth described the challenge in this manner: "An assistant professor can advocate free love, divestiture of South African stocks, abortion on demand, the cessation of all nuclear research, or any number of other things. Chairs and deans have less freedom to say what they think. Presidents have almost none."[58]

In many ways, the leadership of Hutchins at Chicago mirrors the ambivalence Laney showed in dealing with challenge and crisis. The faculty seemed genuinely grateful for Hutchins' impassioned and forceful defense of academic freedom when the critics attacked the university. However, he failed completely in engaging faculty in discussion of issues facing the institution, which in itself became a cause for challenge and crisis. Rather than deal with faculty directly on matters, he showed an arrogance and "conviction of righteousness," according to Dzuback, that created persistent problems for him.[59] While Laney would not be accused of self-righteous behavior, his pattern of response to certain issues, such as apartheid, made those issues seem more urgent and difficult than may have been necessary.

A second pattern demonstrated by Laney's dealings with challenge and crisis was the invocation of the time-honored traditions of the university as a defense. This was evident, for instance, in his response to challenges about the sale of pornographic literature in the university bookstore, about the need to explore the issues of apartheid, about the practices of tenure, and about the need for a multi-cultural presence on campus. It was also used in Strickland's memo concerning the trustees' position on the Great Park, a position most certainly blessed by Laney in advance, if not written by a member of Laney's staff. In these defenses he showed no ambivalence, and was an articulate spokesman for the practice of academic freedom. Eliot used a similar rationale in his support of Catholics at Harvard, and Hutchins did likewise with the external challenges to the curriculum at Chicago. Even when it might have been easier to have done otherwise, such as ban the sale of pornographic material in the bookstore, Laney stood by the central principles of the university.

Finally, despite the ambivalence Laney demonstrated in his handling of some of these issues, it can still be argued that he showed his commitment to moral leadership and moral community in how he addressed them. While Laney's response to the divestment recommendation can be judged as equivocal, his desire to gather members of the Emory community in a cross-constituent conversation about apartheid is laudable. Based on his comments about the process cited earlier, Laney certainly viewed the outcome of the conversations positively. His moral leadership was especially evident in his handling of the racial episodes of 1987 and 1990. Laney's capacity to listen, affirm the concerns of others, articulate thoughtful statements of response, and initiate programs to address the concerns were moments of moral leadership. Laney's encounter of these difficult episodes affected him greatly. According to one of his senior staff, for nearly two months Laney did nothing but deal with the Collins case.[60] A more insecure president might have pointed the finger at Collins and attributed the problems to her. Instead, Laney protected her and her family, never making public mention of the findings of the GBI, and having the university pay for all her medical bills and loss of personal property.[61]

In his handling of these issues, Laney practiced what he preached about the need for moral discourse and the model it serves for students. In discussing the moral dimensions of presidential leadership, he said: "Maybe it is part of the university's role to help socialize those who will be leading society tomorrow. Maybe it is our task to uphold a certain kind of moral decency. This has to be done with extraordinary sensitivity. We cannot do it by fiat or imposition...."[62] Through his leadership on these issues, Laney was demonstrating what Hutchins, some forty years earlier, believed was most needed in academic presidents:

> Men [sic] who possess and practice the virtues are rare enough. Good men who are good philosophers are rarer still. Good men who are good philosophers and who are willing to run the extraordinary occupational hazards, moral and mental, of university administration, are a race which appears to be extinct. Yet if I were asked what single thing American education needed most, I should reply that it needed such men; for the whole system of American education is losing itself for the lack of them.[63]

Not only did Laney give leadership that held the community together during these difficult episodes, but he demonstrated that he, too, learned from them. In his remarks to the Board of Visitors at their annual meeting in mid-May of the year of the Collins case, Laney spent the majority of his speech discussing the impact of the events on the life of the university. He noted that the world was changing in significant ways, as evidenced by the fall of the Berlin Wall and the end of the Cold War. He used these changes as a metaphor that the "old coordinates no longer work. We have to find a new perspective to work from." He noted that simply having numbers of a particular race is not enough to provide inclusion for people. Instead, he said: "Those new coordinates we need must be fashioned out of the frustrating and frequently painful experience of our bumping up against each other's singularity, each other's differences".[64] In all, Laney dealt in a very humane and caring way with a critical institutional moment by demonstrating openness and a pastoral sensitivity—moral leadership—when the time called for it. The files contain many letters thanking Laney for a job well done under difficult and thankless circumstances. One letter from a faculty member expressed the opinion of many when he wrote: "What looked like a sad blot in our University is turning out to be an opportunity for renewed, affirmative progress. We owe that to your leadership and I want to express our gratitude."[65]

---

[1]See, for instance, James L. Fisher and James V. Koch, *Presidential Leadership: Making a Difference* (Phoenix: Oryx Press, 1996) 165–67.

[2]Hugh Hawkins, *Between Harvard and America: The Educational Leadership of Charles W. Eliot* (New York: Oxford University Press, 1991) 185–87.

[3]Richard Storr, *Harper's University: The Beginning* (Chicago: University of Chicago Press, 1966) 223, 254ff.

[4]Mary Ann Dzuback, *Robert M. Hutchins: Portrait of an Educator* (Chicago: University of Chicago Press, 1991) 163–65.

[5]Wayne J. Urban, *Black Scholar: Horace Mann Bond 1904–1972* (Athens: University of Georgia Press, 1992) 122, 130–31, 134–37.

[6]Dzuback, *Robert M. Hutchins*, 165, 227.

[7]Urban, *Black Scholar*, 137. Bond alleged that race was a factor in his removal from office, a matter with which Eliot, Harper, Hutchins, and Laney never had to contend.

[8]For a reprint of the address see James T. Laney, *Our Mission in Higher Education: Vision and Reality* in Presidential Papers, vol. 8, no. 3 (Nashville: Division of Higher Education and Ministry, Board of Higher Education and Ministry, September 1992).

[9]For a reprint of the address see James T. Laney, "How is Jesus the Lord of History," Joe Hale, ed., *Proceedings of the Sixteenth World Methodist Conference* (Lake Junaluska NC: World Methodist Council, 1992).

[10]Among the governing structures of the United Methodist Church is the annual conference. Although Emory is affiliated with the United Methodist Church

through the Southeastern Jurisdiction, comprised of the eighteen annual conferences in the southeast, Emory is physically located in the North Georgia Conference. Annual conferences—headed by bishops—are subdivided into districts, and led by district superintendents. Bishops and district superintendents comprise the cabinet of the annual conference. Along with the help of district superintendents, bishops have authority to appoint clergy who serve United Methodist churches. While Glenn Memorial United Methodist Church is located on the Emory campus, it is considered a church of the North Georgia Conference, giving the bishop the final determination of who serves that congregation.

[11]In 1975, Laney was one of twenty-four clergy elected by his peers to represent the North Georgia Annual Conference at the 1976 quadrennial meeting of the Southeastern Jurisdictional Conference. In 1979, Laney was one of twelve clergy elected by his peers to represent the North Georgia Annual Conference at the 1980 quadrennial meetings of the General Conference (a national body) and the Southeastern Jurisdictional Conference. Laney's election in 1979 was a measure of the growth in his stature among his peers after his appointment as president. He failed to win reelection in 1983 and in subsequent quadrennial elections, in part, I believe, because of his stand on issues. It is also likely that his dealings with the church over controversial concerns made Laney less interested in being elected.

[12]James T. Laney to Colleagues in Ministry, 16 November 1979, Laney Papers, box 16, folder "Pub," RWWL, 1. The United Methodist Church, through its Social Principles, encourages abstinence from alcohol consumption.

[13]"A Pub at Emory," *Atlanta Journal and Constitution Magazine*, 1 April 1979, 6.

[14]See Laney Papers, box 16, folder "Pub," RWWL.

[15]James T. Laney to Colleagues in Ministry, 2.

[16]Ann Hardie, "Volunteer, Nunn Urges Graduates," *Atlanta Journal and Constitution*, 16 May 1989, B3.

[17]See Laney Papers, box 27-1, folder "Commencement 1989," RWWL.

[18]Carl G. Renfroe to James T. Laney, 18 May 1989, Laney Papers, box 27-1, folder "Commencement 1989," RWWL.

[19]James T. Laney to Carl G. Renfroe, 8 June 1989, Laney Papers, box 27-1, folder "Commencement 1989," RWWL, 1.

[20]See Laney Papers, box 21-2, folder "Campus Life," RWWL.

[21]James T. Laney to Bishop Lloyd Knox, 26 September 1986, Laney Papers, box 21-2, folder "Campus Life," RWWL, 1.

[22]In support of Laney's position, it should be noted that the church also had a stand that the civil rights of homosexuals should be guaranteed. This stand was persuasive in Laney's thinking and the action he took, despite the reservation of more conservative-minded trustees about the matter.

[23]Henry M. Bullock, *A History of Emory University* (Nashville: Parthenon Press, 1936) 302–303.

[24]The committee was also charged with other responsibilities, namely to review the work of the Candler School of Theology and the office of campus minister in relation to how these two areas promoted the role of the United Methodist Church on the Emory campus. Members of the committee were Dr. Jim L. Waits (chair), John W. Gilbert, Jr., Paul Anderson, Betty Asbury, Bishop James M. Ault, the Reverend Larry B. Caywood (pastor of Glenn Memorial), Dr. David Graybeal, Bishop Joel D. McDavid, Charles H. McTier, the Reverend Helen Neinast, the Reverend Don Shockley, Dr. Wytch Stubbs, Dr. Judson C. Ward, the Reverend Dr. Will Willimon (dean of the Duke University Chapel).

[25]"Committee on the Church's Presence at Emory University," no date, Laney Papers, box 58, "Glenn Memorial Notebook, 1 of 2," RWWL, 3–4.

[26]Bishop Eugene Frank to James T. Laney, 13 March 1989, Laney files, box 58, "Glenn Memorial Notebook, 1 of 2," RWWL.

[27]J. Thomas Bertrand, July 1997, copyrighted personal notes, Brevard NC, in author's possession.

[28]"Emory, the Carter Center and the Issue of the Roadway Through the Great Park: A Chronology," not dated, Laney Papers, box 23-3, "Correspondence Notebook April–June 1986," RWWL, 1–3. The reader should not be confused by the location of this document in Laney's correspondence notebook. The thirteen year diary was filed in Laney's correspondence notebook for the months April–June 1986.

[29]James T. Laney to the Emory Faculty, 16 January 1982, Laney Papers, box 23-2, "Correspondence Notebook April–June 1986," RWWL.

[30]"Resolution Proposed by Professor Dan Carter," no date, Laney Papers, box 23-2, "Correspondence Notebook April–June 1986," RWWL.

[31]"Emory, the Carter Center and the Issue of the Roadway," 3.

[32]Robert Strickland to Those Concerned, 29 January 1985, Laney Papers, box 23-3, "Correspondence Notebook April–June 1986," RWWL.

[33]James T. Laney, interview by author, tape recording, Emory University, Atlanta, 17 August 1998. Laney said that "he had a lot of explaining to do" to Carter over the faculty response.

[34]The Sullivan Principles were written in 1975 by the Rev. Leon Sullivan and first adopted in 1977 by major US corporations. The principles called for corporations to: integrate all company facilities; establish equal and fair employment practices; offer equal pay for employees performing equal work; develop training programs for nonwhites; increase the number of black managers; and improve housing, transportation, education, and health facilities for employees. See Jonathan

Leape, Bo Baskin, and Stefan Underhill, *Business in the Shadow of Apartheid: US Firms in South Africa* (Lexington MA: D. C. Heath and Company, 1985) 217–18.

[35]James T. Laney to Bishop Joel McDavid, 11 September 1985, Laney Papers, box 21-2, folder "South Africa," RWWL, 1.

[36]James T. Laney to Bishop Joel McDavid.

[37]James T. Laney, "Presidential Leadership for Shared Values in Pluralist Communities: The Issue and the Challenge," January 1991, *Heart*, 27. See also James T. Laney, "Through Thick and Thin: Two Ways of Talking about the Academy and Moral Responsibility," in *Ethics in Higher Education*, ed. William W. May (New York: American Council on Education, 1990) 62–63.

[38]Laney, "Presidential Leadership for Shared Values," 27.

[39]James T. Laney to Roberto Goizeuta and Don Keough, 18 July 1986, Laney Papers, box 21-2, folder "South Africa," RWWL, 1–2.

[40]Laney, "Through Thick and Thin," 62.

[41]"Minutes of the Investment Committee of the Board of Trustees of Emory University," 14 July 1987, Laney Papers, box 10, folder "BOT Misc.," RWWL. John Temple, executive vice president for Emory at the time, explained in an interview that the university never divested of any of its stock. John Temple, interview by author, note recording, Emory University, Atlanta, 17 July 1998.

[42]See Laney Papers, box 4, folder "Equal Opportunity Program," RWWL.

[43]Folder "Equal Opportunity Program," Laney Papers.

[44]James T. Laney to the Emory Students, Faculty and Staff, 19 November 1987, Laney Papers, box 4, folder "Equal Opportunity Program," RWWL, 2.

[45]Laney to the Emory Students, Faculty and Staff, 19 November 1987, Laney Papers.

[46]The matter also received national attention. See "Racial Attacks Leave Freshman in Severe Shock," *New York Times*, 22 April 1990, I-44.

[47]For all these materials see Laney Papers, box 38, folder "Collins, Sabrina," RWWL.

[48]"Statement of the African American Students of Emory University," no date, Laney Papers, box 38, folder "Collins, Sabrina," RWWL.

[49]James T. Laney, "A Letter from President Laney to the Emory Community," 17 April 1990, Laney Papers, box 38, folder "Collins, Sabrina," RWWL. At the time of issuing this letter, Laney was aware of the conclusions of the GBI about the case. Laney's visit to Augusta to visit Collins' family while she was in the hospital occurred on Easter Sunday.

[50]"Remarks by President James T. Laney to Students, Sunday Evening, April 22," 22 April (no year), Laney Papers, box 38, folder "Collins, Sabrina," RWWL, 1–2.

[51]"Remarks by President James T. Laney to Students, Sunday Evening, April 22," Laney Papers, 4–5.

[52]"An Open Letter to the Atlanta Community Concerning Emory University: Draft," no date, Laney Papers, box 38, folder "Collins, Sabrina," RWWL, 1.

[53]Frances B. Milton to James T. Laney, 23 April 1990, Laney Papers, box 38, folder "Collins, Sabrina," RWWL.

[54]S.F. Silversmith to James T. Laney, 25 July 1990, Laney Papers, box 38, folder "Collins, Sabrina," RWWL.

[55]Bradd Shore to James T. Laney, 19 April 1990, Laney Papers, box 38, folder "Collins, Sabrina," RWWL.

[56]James T. Laney to Robert Strickland, 30 April 1990, Laney Papers, box 6-8, pt. 3, "Correspondence Notebook April–June 1990," RWWL, 2.

[57]Laney interview, 17 August 1998. In this interview, Laney said he once told a colleague about the apartheid issue and his commitment to it, "Where else in the country do you have the president out in front of the student body?"

[58]Jean Kemeny, *It's Different at Dartmouth* (Brattleboro VT: Stephen Greene Press, 1979) 22.

[59]Dzuback, *Robert M. Hutchins*, 207.

[60]Temple interview.

[61]William H. Fox, interview by author, note recording, Emory University, Atlanta, 7 July 1998.

[62]James T. Laney, "The Moral Authority of the President," April 1983, *Heart*, 7–8.

[63]Robert Maynard Hutchins, *Freedom, Education and the Fund: Essays and Addresses, 1946–1956* (New York: Meridan Books, 1956) 179.

[64]James T. Laney, "President Laney's Speech to the Emory University Board of Visitors," 16 May 1990, Laney Papers, box 25-1, pocket 6, RWWL, 1–2.

[65]Bill and Gatra Mallard to James T. Laney, 25 April 1990, Laney Papers, box 38, folder "Collins, Sabrina," RWWL.

CHAPTER SIX

LANEY AS MORAL LEADER
The Essential Ingredients for Effective Leadership

While numerous theories of leadership in higher education have been advanced, the large number of theories suggest that no one view about leadership is applicable to all academic presidents. The leadership of Laney at Emory, or of Hutchins at Chicago, or of any president at any institution demonstrates that no one theory in higher education adequately captures the essence of what it takes to be an effective president. Despite the differences in leadership style and philosophy exercised by academic presidents, the Weberian category of positional authority is applicable to all academic leaders. Laney's exercise of leadership in the context of the bureaucracy and network of voluntary followers at Emory demonstrated that the leadership exercised is fundamentally moral.

Examining the backgrounds of academic presidents, including age, gender, race, nationality, religious background, socioeconomic background, educational attainment, sexual orientation, and disabilities, it is clear that leaders are a diverse lot, at least as far as their demographic make-up is concerned. Laney for instance was forty-nine years of age when appointed president of Emory; Hutchins was a mere thirty. Laney was an internal appointment, while Hutchins was an external appointment, having come from Yale law school. Laney was a theologian and ethicist by training; Hutchins was a lawyer. Despite these differences in backgrounds, the one inescapable condition for leadership in higher education that all presidents share is that they have voluntary followers in a given context. Thus, while presidents may have differing backgrounds, personalities and gene pools, the one and only condition they all share in common is that they exercise authority in settings that have followers who give their allegiance voluntarily. The allegiance granted by followers to leaders must be voluntary, and not coerced or forced, for leadership can only exist within a context where the leader is freely chosen and allegiance freely granted by the followers.[1] Although Weber did not write about leadership in higher education, his foundational insights about leadership generally have influenced much of the thinking about leadership in higher education today. Weber understood well the role of the context in creating and forming leaders. He believed that voluntary submission to imperative control, when legitimate, is based on three grounds: rational, traditional, and charismatic.[2]

Rational or positional authority, according to Weber, is that granted to an individual by organizations and institutions which are fundamentally bureaucratic in nature. The person in the position of authority is charged with achieving the goals of the institution. Followers show allegiance to this person because she/he is the organization's designated leader. Traditional authority is based on "the sanctity of the order" and the powers of control as they have been passed down over the years. In traditional authority, authority is based on loyalty to the leader, unlike positional authority where authority is based on the position of the leader. Charismatic authority is that power given to an individual by the followers because of the extraordinary qualities of the leader, which are often considered divinely ordained.[3] Most leadership is of the positional authority variety. Instances of traditional and charismatic authority are rare, especially so in the United States. Seldom does one find traditional or charismatic authority in evidence in this country in business, government, non-profit agencies, or the church.

Given these Weberian categories, one can conclude that presidents of US colleges and universities come to their positions not because of tradition or charisma, but because they are freely selected by a group of the institution's followers.[4] This is not to say that elements of traditional and charismatic authority cannot be found in higher education, for often followers in higher education settings will grant their allegiance to the leader because of traditions in the institution or because of some charisma in the leader the follower finds appealing. But nearly always, the allegiance is granted on the basis of the position held by the leader. Over time, the charisma of the leader, as it becomes evident to the followers, may be an even more significant element in the allegiance of the followers than the fact that the leader happens to be president, as was true for both Laney and Hutchins. Although charisma is an important attribute that enables a leader to perform effectively, it is not an attribute shared by all leaders of higher education settings. Thus, the only claim that can be made about presidents in higher education settings is that they are freely chosen to lead in these settings and that they have colleagues, or followers, who grant them their allegiance freely. This following rests fundamentally on the moral standards exercised by the president.

Chapter 1 detailed the circumstances of the search that led to the hiring of Laney as president of Emory in 1977. While there may be some historical disagreement about how open that search really was—for example, did the trustee search committee take as seriously as the faculty committee the other candidates under consideration, or did they intend all along to accept Woodruff's wish to appoint Laney—the fact is that Laney was selected under circumstances and conditions considered customary in higher education at the time. While faculty and staff had the option of resigning their positions in protest to his appointment, so far as the record shows no one did. In fact, there seemed to be excitement and hopefulness at what he could do for Emory, giving him, then, a setting where there were followers who gave their allegiance freely to the leadership attributes he exercised.

Within the higher education setting, the president is the one charged by trustees and other constituents to formulate and articulate a vision for the institution. Followers adhere to a leader because of the goals and direction she/he has identified for the future of the institution. The leader's vision, while future oriented, has its roots in the history and traditions of the institution. Only by understanding the past of the followers in the organization can the leader move the followers into the future. A vision answers the *who?*, *what?*, *when?*, *where?*, *how?*, and *why?* questions of the followers and the institution. Among the questions the leader seeks to answer are these: Whom does the institution serve? How might it better and more effectively offer its services? Why does it exist?

The vision of the president must keep touch with all the environments that impinge on the institution. Thus, constant communication with all constituent groups, including faculty, students, staff, trustees, graduates, and supporters, ensures that the president articulates a vision that inspires them and motivates their following from their limited perspective to the larger good of the institution. Laney expressed the challenge:

> I am convinced that we have come to a time in our institutional history when it is no longer adequate for each of these segments of the university to feel that they are accountable or loyal only to their limited interests.... [M]odern society and its institutions tend constantly toward the minimization of participation, and the result is alienation, with its attendant suspicion and skepticism and uncertainty and sense of distance. The president must constantly battle to overcome this downward pull, to get faculty and staff and students and alumni to feel that they have a stake in the whole. This may be our greatest task.[5]

A leader in higher education, then, is one whose vision gains the confidence and support of followers in all constituent groups. As Ault notes, the vision of the president is fundamentally relational in that without a vision the leader will have no followers.[6]

If nothing else, the chapters up to this point have demonstrated that an outstanding characteristic of Laney's presidency was his ability to articulate a vision and gain the support of others. In developing his vision for Emory, Laney was aided in his experience with and knowledge of the great universities of this country, especially Yale. As a student at Yale, and later a member of the Visiting Committee of the Harvard Divinity School, Laney had a firm grasp of what a liberal arts education should be and what it took to become a great, national university. His knowledge of what needed to happen at Emory was aided by his eight years there as dean of the Candler School of Theology before ascending to the presidency. He had an inner knowledge of the history and dynamics that had made Emory what it was, a knowledge that someone from the outside might have learned in time, but would have been initially handicapped in not knowing. Laney also anticipated the growth that would occur in Atlanta and took advantage of this fact by arguing for a "great university in a great city." In each of these instances, Ault contends that Laney's grasp of the potentialities inherent at Emory made him an effective visionary.[7]

Laney clearly knew how to articulate his vision to gain the support of others. For instance, the Woodruff brothers responded in an extraordinary way with their magnanimous gift. Laney was unabashed in the confidence he felt about the vision, as when he challenged the "provincial loyalty and Southern pride" of the trustees at their 1987 retreat by saying that it was "intolerable" that the South could not claim to have a leading private university among the nation's most elite.

Laney succeeded with much of the faculty throughout the university in gaining their support of his vision, especially in the first phase of his administration when he laid out his view of Emory's future. Following his 1979 report to the faculty, for instance, Laney received rave responses. A professor of theology wrote, "You helped me and doubtless many others to feel a genuine part of a university yesterday. It is the first time since I began teaching that I've sensed a kind of internal ownership." A psychology professor wrote, "Your report to the faculty was superb. Congrats and right on!" A law professor said, "Your presentation…was virtually inspiring." A chemistry professor exclaimed, "It is clear to me that I will see the greatness that Emory is destined to realize during my academic lifetime."[8]

In reflecting on Laney's capacity to create a vision and move the institution forward, his provost offered this reflection:

> Perhaps his greatest contribution was to help us see in Emory the possibility of greatness, to raise our expectations of ourselves, and to set a higher standard of hope and achievement. The result is that during the past 15 years we have seen a veritable metamorphosis of Emory from a very fine regional university primarily devoted to teaching, into a university that is recognized nationally and internationally for excellence in scholarship and graduate education as well as teaching.[9]

Time and again in interviews with those who worked closely with Laney, his former colleagues marvel at his capacity to convey a vision. They describe him as being tough-minded, imaginative, creative, and persuasive in the conveying of that message.[10] The Laney files are filled with letters from appreciative listeners who heard him articulate his thoughts on the importance of a liberal arts education and what Emory was doing to achieve it.

Although those close to the university seemed to respond positively to the vision Laney advanced for Emory's future, it is not entirely clear to what extent those close to the university were invited by Laney to help in determining what that vision would be. Earlier it was noted that Laney felt it appropriate to involve others in the determination of the institution's vision. The evidence would suggest in Laney's case, however, that the vision he articulated, albeit appropriate for Emory, was his alone. While he named committees to assist in the setting of priorities for the institution, especially in preparation for the two capital campaigns of his administration, and while he insisted on an internal and external review of the entire university after the Woodruff gift was realized, there is no evidence that Laney sought the opinion of others in what the university's vision should be. In fact, administrative colleagues noted that they thought Laney knew the outcomes of these reports before they were submitted. In an intuitive way, Laney knew what it would take to accomplish his vision for the university.[11] The use of committee participation from time to time was to give the semblance of participation in the decision making and to strengthen his hand for the consequences his vision and decisions might have.

That Laney had the vision himself is evidenced by his comments about the early days of his administration. In reflecting on what was achieved at Emory during his tenure, he described it as a "period of building...to chart the course of the university...in a fresh way. In a sense to take stock of what *I* [italics author's] thought higher education should accomplish and to try to implement that vision." Thus, Laney's task became one of educating the community about that vision, which he viewed as an important element of presidential leadership. He said, "...a president ought to know enough of what they are doing, in terms of their leadership, to educate."[12] He remembers his inaugural address as a time when he attempted to edify the gathering about the common project

before the various constituents of the institution to create a community
of scholars. He went on to observe:

> We may have different tasks, but the power of the uni-
> versity came from that synergy released in the process of
> dialogue and interdisciplinary discussions and mutual
> edification. I thought I ought to be *primus inter pares*,
> not the top, but just the first among equals, simply by
> virtue of my role. I was quite unabashed in making it
> clear that was my role, that I saw it that way. Not aggres-
> sively, but, I think, with some constancy and I hope, at
> least in time, confidence.[13]

In addition to the vision articulated by the president, a second
attribute that Laney showed to be important is the ability to tolerate
ambiguity. With diverse constituent groups and varying agendas, ambiguity in the complex organization of the university is inevitable. Cohen
and March have described the life of an academic president as "organized
anarchy" because the university is characterized by problematic goals,
unclear technology, and fluid participation. They explain the tension in
this manner:

> ...presidents discover that they have less power than is
> believed, that their power to accomplish things depends
> heavily on what they want to accomplish, that the use of
> formal authority is limited by other formal authority,
> that the acceptance of authority is not automatic, that
> the necessary details of organizational life confuse power
> (which is somewhat different from diffusing it), and that
> their colleagues seem to delight in complaining simulta-

neously about presidential weakness and presidential willfulness.[14]

Learning to manage ambiguity is critical for the president to exercise her/his power and authority, according to Cohen and March.

For Cohen and March, a leader is one who approaches the ambiguity of her/his work with great humility for the opportunities and limitations provided by the office of president. According to Cohen and March, a humble president will use the following eight tactical rules to exercise her/his leadership: (1) spend time on decisions to be made so that she/he will be a major information source; (2) persist; (3) exchange status for substance; (4) facilitate opposition participation; (5) overload the system; (6) provide garbage cans; (7) manage unobtrusively; and (8) interpret history.[15] Use of these tactical rules is crucial to maintain the momentum of the organization and avoid the inclination toward what Simon called "satisficing." Building on Simon's term, Plous explains that the complexity and ambiguity of the organization can cause the leader and followers to make choices and decisions that are satisfactory and sufficient but not optimal. In the long-term, decisions based on satisficing dilute the effectiveness of the organization.[16]

Laney's experience as president demonstrated the tremendous ambiguity that comes with a large university. The challenges he faced in his sixteen years are good examples of this ambiguity that exist within and among all the institution's constituent groups, including the church, faculty, trustees, corporations, and students. Yet, Laney's experience also proves that ambiguity in the organization does not have to be as limiting as Cohen and March suggest it can be. For Laney, the way to overcome the limits of ambiguity was to be clear about the vision and articulate the clarity of vision in as broadly and in as compelling a way as possible. Laney expressed his opinion about ambiguity in the organization:

The president, obviously, is very constrained, but, you know, you're the one that signs off on the appointments, signs off on the budget. You've got some real leverage. The question is whether you can articulate a vision that can mobilize people. I've never known leadership to be different than that at any time. People are always busy doing their thing, and the only way they ever follow anybody is because they think that's the way you've got to go....The university is complex, and it's not a simple straight line operation.[17]

Curiously, Laney found ways to make the ambiguity of the university work for him. In some cases, he created ambiguity himself. Senior staff recall that Laney was not wedded to administrative structures and chain-of-command authority. He simply wanted the job done. His means of getting the job done was to hire the best people possible and turn them loose on their responsibilities. Staff were left to sort through the building up of their offices and negotiating their responsibilities with their administrative colleagues.[18]

Frye remembers that when he was appointed to the newly created office of provost in 1987, he inherited no structure from which to work. Armed with only an assistant, Frye had to build his operation from scratch, keeping Laney informed about the development of the office, but assuming that he was fulfilling the charge that Laney had given him.[19] Thomas Bertrand, Laney's secretary of the university, and Fox recall that the ambiguity in roles of his senior staff created an atmosphere—albeit tense and "maddening" at times—that would ultimately foster creativity and solutions. Bertrand had this to say about one of Laney's greatest attributes: "[Laney resisted] a chain-of-command kind of organization. He hired outstanding individuals with strong personalities and let them define their own turfs. This has been a real challenge for some individuals who want more direction, more structure, but it has created an atmosphere where imagination and initiative are encouraged."[20]

John Temple, Laney's executive vice president for finance, said that Laney never seemed bothered when his administrative staff was knocking heads with each other over a decision or a particular responsibility. He said Laney just seemed to ignore the confusion, trusting that the proper decision would be made.[21] For Laney, this practice was intentional, and could be described by those critical of Laney as manipulative. Laney said his model in this style of leadership was President Franklin D. Roosevelt, who, according to Laney, "used people of enormous ability but would never let them feel secure in their jobs."[22] The downside of such leadership is that the leader may appear devious and power hungry, but for Laney the creativity and willingness to risk such an appearance, fostered among the staff, was his motivation for operating in this fashion. Reflecting on his leadership style and the tension and the ambiguity it created, Laney had this to say:

> I have a deep conviction, and it has not changed— having served in government and watched the church, or anything else—that you wind up with people protecting their turf, but more than that, the main thing is you avoid blame. Because nobody wants to make a decision that is risky, and we were living in an age of risk. Everything we did was risky.... But I wanted that tension, and it was very deliberate. We had to keep a sense of parsimony and prudence, even at the time we are trying to be very adventurous and innovative. Now, those are hard to mesh. That's why I did it.[23]

Laney's tolerance for this kind of ambiguity among his staff was aided by his strong sense of confidence both about his vision for Emory and about the caliber of staff he had hired. Ault contends that Laney was a masterful leader because he was an outstanding manager of staff. He notes that Laney appointed very different people with the gifts and skills appropriate for the tasks for which they were hired. Through proper staffing, Laney was able to handle the varied agendas and sensibilities of the university's numerous constituencies.[24] Administrative colleagues and trustees also remember that much of Laney's ability to tolerate ambiguity was confidence in his own judgments on matters. This confidence enabled him not to be threatened by those who might oppose him.[25]

Laney's presidency exhibits a third important ingredient in moral leadership, and that is a commitment to teamwork. In recent years especially, teamwork has become a focus of the presidential leadership literature, most notably in the writings of Bensimon and Neumann. These writers argue that prior to their study on teams in higher education scholars tended to view leadership as an individual act sustained by hierarchical relationships. In their revised notion of leadership, Bensimon and Neumann see teamwork as a highly collective and interactive process. From this standpoint, then, a leader is one who involves others in the decision making process, especially those who are on the margin of the organization.[26] Bensimon and Neumann hold that there are several key implications to their notion of teamwork. First is that leaders make themselves open to having their views on a subject challenged and changed. Second is that leaders are willing to respect those who understand and interpret reality differently from themselves. Both implications are crucial to leaders because they are helped to avoid what Plous calls selective perception. According to Plous, leaders are naturally inclined to perceive what they want to hear.[27] Teamwork that includes representative voices from the organization can minimize the selective perception of the leader. While a teamwork orientation to leadership is much more time consuming and potentially can lead to group-think,[28] the advocates of such an approach believe that the conscientious leader will be attentive to these dangers and steer the team away from them.

Laney's use of a team approach during his tenure at Emory is more like the hierarchical teamwork model Bensimon and Neumann describe and oppose, and less like the model they advocate. Still, he was not oblivious to the points these teamwork advocates espouse. With his concern about the moral dimensions of education and his own Christian ethics background, Laney knew and understood the importance of those on the margin having their rightful voice in the decision making of the institution. He demonstrated this in the deft handling of the racial issues Emory faced, especially in 1990. He was a champion for many of the issues raised by the Commission on Minorities, Commission on Women, which was started during his administration, and the Employee Council, all groups with which he met on a regular basis. In 1993, he saw to it that sexual orientation was added to the university's Equal Opportunity Statement, which came at a high political price, according to Ault.[29]

Given Laney's demonstrated openness on a number of issues affecting those on the margin of the university, it should be noted that he did not have among his vice presidential colleagues for the majority of his tenure anything other than white, male leadership. Not until the very end of his tenure did he appoint a woman and African-American male to vice presidential posts. The absence of these voices from his major policy making staff during most of his administration leave open the question of whether the voices of those on the margin of the organization were adequately represented. Could, for instance, the racial turmoil of 1990 have been avoided had there been African-Americans at the very senior level, advising Laney about the climate for African-American students on campus?

The absence of a more representative administrative staff in Laney's administration raises questions about his commitment to Bensimon and

Neumann's view of teamwork, as does his handling of staff meetings. Senior staff remember that staff meetings were occasions to discuss issues, but the advising was almost always for the purpose of aiding Laney in making key decisions. While there were many issues facing the university on which the senior staff did reach consensus, there was never a doubt that Laney was the final arbiter in all matters, which leads one to wonder whether Laney was truly the *primus inter pares*, as he saw himself. Frye gave this understanding about Laney's openness to and working relationship with his senior staff, which also speaks to Laney's sense of self-confidence and his ability to handle ambiguity:

> He was also impatient. The extent to which he was willing to participate in any…conversation was limited. But I think he was reasonably encouraging of that kind of deliberation. You always have to remember that, for him, if it was some big issue, he had not only us to contend with, but he had trustees and other interest groups. And how many times can you talk about the same problem before you say, "The buck stops here"? He was never shy about that that I know of. Again, he accepted his responsibility as president with great courage and confidence.[30]

Perhaps the constituent group which displayed the most consternation with Laney's leadership was the faculty. While there is evidence in the files that faculty resistance to some of Laney's decisions surfaced as early as 1979, the tension was especially pronounced by the time of his departure in 1993. One of Laney's senior staff observed that had Laney remained there would have needed to have been a fundamental shift in leadership style, if nothing else to placate the faculty.[31] One of the first signs of dissatisfaction with Laney's lack of team approach and consultation came two years after his appointment, when he unilaterally promoted the dean of the college to become vice president for academic affairs. In response, Jack Boozer, co-chair of the Emory AAUP Committee on Governance, wrote these comments to Laney: "Because of your earlier statements and actions the recent appointments at the Vice Presidential level, with limited or no consultation with the faculties most affected by these appointments, surprised and alarmed us....[It] contradicted the principle of consultation and compromised the faculty support with which the appointee might enter the new position."[32] In behalf of the committee, Boozer requested that members have a meeting with Laney to discuss the issues further. This meeting was held in October. Minutes of the meeting show that Laney held his ground on his right to use whatever means he deemed appropriate for the appointment of vice presidential staff. Laney made a distinction between vice presidents and deans, the latter being "the primary academic officers of the university." In appointment of deans, Laney pledged to use search committees and every means possible to develop broad consensus on the appointees. Laney's primary point in the meeting, however, was that teamwork, consultation, and collegiality should center on the academic mission of the institution, not the staff hired. The minutes stated his opinion like this: "...President Laney expressed a strong desire for an informal, constructive debate with and among the faculty which would increase collegial involvement in intellectual inquiry and nurture the unity of the University around intellectual concerns, concerns which are logically prior to administrative organization and the special missions of different schools and divisions."[33]

Laney's position on vice presidential appointments was no doubt prompted by the failure of the search committee process he had employed in the discovery of his first significant vice presidential appointment, Carroll Moulton, as vice president for campus life. Because of the tremendous needs in campus life, as noted earlier, Laney made this area his top priority. Wanting as much involvement of constituents in the process as possible, Laney empowered the search committee to identify the person to be appointed. Within two months of the arrival of Moulton on campus, it was evident to many students and faculty, and Laney himself, that the appointment would not work. Moulton eventually resigned. William Fox was named an interim vice president, and was permanently appointed to the position in 1981. Laney reflected on this episode in this way: "Search committees can be helpful, but they can't take the place of your own judgment. Don't remand to the committee. From then on [after the Moulton appointment], I never let a committee choose. I let them present three people unranked, so I was not at the mercy of having to go down the line of first, second, third, because then, in fact, they made the choice."[34]

Laney's approach to this manner of using search committees resulted in at least one instance of considerable faculty frustration in early 1990 when Laney rejected a candidate recommended for the dean's position in the college to succeed Minter. Members of the committee felt that Laney had charged them with a fair and democratic process in the selection of this person, and that Laney's rejection of their nominee, in whom they had great confidence, was autocratic. In writing to Provost Frye about the matter, several members of the search committee had this to say:

> ...faculty morale is very low right now: if Emory University is ever to be the kind of community that you and President Laney and all of us want it to be, the faculty need more than formulaic statements to assure them that their voices are heard and that they themselves are more than mere employees of this place.[35]
>
> If the administration is going to use a "democratic" mechanism for selecting the dean, it behooves it to live with the consequences of such an approach.... There is no need to be "democratic" in the search for a dean, but

pretending to, to a population of Ph.D.'s does create resentment and corrode morale.[36]

In defense of Laney from these attacks, Frye noted that a distinction must be made between consultation and decision making. To accept the recommendation of a committee, about which the president does not feel comfortable, would be for the president to abdicate her/his responsibility. As Frye noted, "The president, if he's got any responsibility other than just being a figurehead, it's got to be veto power."[37]

Laney took very seriously the appointment of his vice presidents and deans. Many of his senior staff related surprise at how Laney found out about them, and about how aggressive he could be in pursuit of the person he believed best suited for the position. Minter remembers that Laney went to Houston to spend the day to convince him to accept the offer of dean of the college.[38] Fox remembers that while he served as vice president of campus life Laney was relentless in his pursuit of him to become vice president for institutional advancement, even though Fox had never had formal fundraising experience. In the case of Fox, Laney was clear that what he needed was someone who knew and loved Emory and who could learn fundraising quickly, rather than the opposite kind of person, who was a professional fundraiser, but had no knowledge of and appreciation for Emory's history, traditions, and mission. An additional gift Fox noted that Laney gave his staff was permission to be their own person, to perform their jobs with authenticity and not conform to a specified way of being and acting.[39]

Despite what might be perceived as a weakness in that Laney operated his team from a hierarchical model, all the senior staff interviewed expressed deep appreciation for Laney's leadership and his support— moral, financial, and otherwise—in allowing them to do their jobs.[40] Laney's staff revered him in a way similar to those who worked with and revered Harper at Chicago. Veysey said that Harper could "infuse his own mastery into the people about him." He goes on to say this about Harper, which was equally true about Laney: "Only on the margins of the faculty, outside the charmed inner circle, was Harper considered an autocrat. More often men believed themselves to be neither cajoled nor coerced by him, but rather compelled by him."[41]

Laney's leadership with the board was not unlike his efforts with the staff. Like his staff, the board, and the executive committee in particular, were for the most part white males. Only one woman was appointed to the executive committee during Laney's tenure, and the remaining members were all white males mostly from Atlanta.[42] Very few major institutional issues were addressed in full board sessions. Most issues were vetted through appropriate committees, and even many of these issues were addressed in informal conversations between Laney and individual trustees. The decision of the executive committee to add sexual orientation to the Equal Opportunity Statement was "prepared" (Laney's term) ahead of time by Laney with visits and telephone calls to key trustees.[43] The reason for doing this, according to Ault, was to respect Southern mores, which attempt to avoid conflict in public settings, especially among older, white men.[44]

Laney enjoyed the full confidence of his board chair, Robert Strickland. Strickland intruded little, if at all, in the operation of the university, according to Laney. Laney kept him briefed on major issues through regular meetings, telephone calls, and occasional memoranda.[45] As he did with staff, Laney was quick to defend himself with trustees on matters where there may have been disagreement. One particularly strong defense of himself found in the files concerns a conversation with a trustee about the trustee's objections to a perceived *quid pro quo* that Laney agreed to in appointing the university's first African-American trustee, Marvin Arrington. In a memorandum to the development office files about the encounter, Laney wrote, "I flatly denied that anything of the sort had occurred, and told him that I thought it was totally inappropriate that people who had known me for this long should charge me with such behavior. I think he became a little sheepish at that point and backed off....Whether that will stop the talk I do not know."[46] For Laney, membership on the team, whether trustee, staff, or faculty, required clarity about who was in charge and what the agenda would be, while, at the same time, allowing himself to be open to the criticisms of others.

While this discussion has noted some disagreements between Laney and the faculty, these are the only evidences of disagreement found in the files. Thus, to surmise on the basis of these few disagreements in sixteen years that Laney had unproductive and unhealthy relationships with faculty and staff would be a mischaracterization. Laney's vision for Emory, his comfort with ambiguity, his personal confidence and his trust of his staff made him an effective and confident team player and leader in the traditional sense. Where Laney and Emory might have benefited more would have been in greater inclusion of women and minorities in the governance of the institution, especially at the administrative and trustee levels.

Much of the literature on leadership in higher education suggests that the personal charisma of the individual is necessary for a successful presidency, and Laney proved this to be true. Unlike the attributes of vision, comfort with ambiguity, and teamwork, *charisma* is among the most difficult attributes to define, for it can mean many things. According to Conger, *charisma* refers to the total person of the leader—her/his personality, appearance, demeanor, oratorical abilities, compassion for others, intelligence, vision, and sense of humor.[47] Fisher and Koch describe a leader with charisma as being "transformational." For them, a transformational leader "provides vision, instills pride, inspires confidence and trust, expresses important goals in simple ways, promotes intelligence, and treats everyone individually."[48] While the strengths of leaders vary dramatically, charisma includes those qualities deemed important by the followers.

In remembering Laney, many of his senior staff describe him in charismatic terms. They refer to his ability to listen, his oratorical skills, his facility with language, his sharp and penetrating mind, his energy, his tenacity, his competitive and entrepreneurial instincts, and his pastoral sensitivities, a combination that made him a rare academic leader. These traits attracted many people to him, and many of his senior staff deemed him the most important and influential figure in their lives. Fox said that other than his mother, Laney had had the most influence on him. Minter said that of all the faculty and staff at Emory, he talked to Laney the most and learned the most from him, even though he did not technically report directly to him. Trustee Sibley described Laney as among his closest personal friends.[49]

Among the charismatic qualities that Laney possessed was the spellbinding nature in which he delivered his speeches. Those who heard him remember with awe the way he engaged his listeners in true preacher-like fashion.[50] Most of his presentations to Emory groups, such as entering students, parents of freshmen, alumni, boards of visitors, and graduating seniors during the baccalaureate service, were not written in advance, but delivered from notes. The written record of these addresses is the result of transcription from tapes of these presentations, which Laney insisted had to be taped for this purpose. Academic presentations, such as convocation speeches and his inaugural address, he wrote himself. Later in his presidency, academic articles and some addresses were authored, in part, by his secretary of the university, Gary Hauk.

Minter remembers Laney best for his sheer intelligence and ability to analyze situations, which came as a result of his ability to listen well to arguments and evidence. Whenever Minter was faced with a challenge in recruiting faculty, he saw to it that the candidates had a private meeting with Laney. The purpose of the meeting was to reassure those skeptical about the university having a preacher as a president; the meeting let them see the interest in and knowledge of a variety of academic disciplines possessed by Laney.[51] Fox remembers that Laney's vocabulary was so large that often he would write down words he heard Laney use in staff meetings, rush to his office and look them up in a dictionary.[52]

Laney's presence was so commanding that he quickly became a peer with those in the Atlanta establishment, many of whom were trustees at Emory. The benefit of being so widely respected, Laney noted, was that it enabled him to move sufficiently in these leaders' world to allow "informal conversation [so that] you can carry on things that don't have to be done so officially."[53] Bertrand notes that Laney "parlayed his brains, his reputation for integrity, his hearty sense of humor, and his understanding of economics into real clout in Atlanta," which he was willing to risk by lecturing the establishment on ethical issues, especially professional ethics, which he gave to guilds of lawyers, doctors, businessmen, and bankers.[54]

Part of what drew others to Laney was his pastoral skill and sensitivity, enhanced by his southern upbringing. He remembered people, expressed interest in their concerns, shared his grief with them when they experienced disappointment or loss and his happiness and pride at a major accomplishment or marker event, such as birthdays and anniversaries. His files are filled with copies of what Bertrand describes as "grace notes"—brief, handwritten notes of support, encouragement, or appreciation. The recipients of these expressions were often amazed that Laney knew or cared about their concerns. Frye points out, however, that Laney was not concerned just to make people feel good by sending these notes nor was he glad-handing. When Laney was dissatisfied by an action or inaction on the part of a staff member, he was quick to express it. In this way, the staff found him very demanding, with extremely high expectations.[55] Yet, the grace notes were a way, according to Laney, of "recognizing a felt obligation" to affirm others' humanity so they will not feel "injured" if it was not recognized.[56]

His personal expressions were not just limited to notes, but included telephone calls and occasionally unannounced visits. Often he used this personal touch to assist in his management of the university and the major issues he faced. Ault recalls a conversation he had with a female associate professor of anthropology who related this instance to him:

> Laney arriv[ed] at her door one day to discuss the controversial decision to deny tenure to the first woman put up for it at Emory. Though Barlett was unhappy with the University's decision, it made a difference in the confidence she felt in the administration that Laney came to talk with her directly about it. It was a moment where the fragile bonds of good faith, trust, and loyalty linking a person with an institution were tried and strengthened.[57]

For all of his warmth and personal interest in faculty, staff, students, trustees, and friends, it is interesting to note that Laney's charisma was enhanced by the distance and formality he maintained in most of his relationships. Almost everyone, including his top aides, referred to him—in public, at least—as "President Laney" or "Dr. Laney." Laney's secretary suggested that this practice was due to Laney's deference to the office of president,[58] or exercising what Fisher and Koch call "the platform" of the presidency.[59] Those skeptical about such practices might conclude that Laney had ego needs which were fed by these titles. Whatever the case, the use of these titles created a power in relationships which permitted Laney to dominate and enabled him to maintain his distance.

A final ingredient that Laney showed which makes for an effective presidency is a commitment to the moral dimensions of the office. The presidential literature is remarkably silent about the importance of the moral commitment of the leader. Yet, what makes Laney's presidency distinctive is his grasp of the moral authority of the president, in an era where integrity seemed in short supply, as evidenced by the unethical behavior of businessmen such as Ivan Boesky, or politicians such as Gary Hart, or preachers such as Jim Bakker. Even the moral foundations of higher education were called into question by people such as William Bennett, Allan Bloom, and Ernest Boyer.[60] Laney seemed to live by the dictum of Martin Luther King, who urged his followers "to create leaders who embody virtues we can respect, who have moral and ethical principles we can applaud with an enthusiasm that enables us to rally support for them with confidence and trust."[61] Since followers give their allegiance voluntarily, they play a crucial role in holding their leaders to a higher standard that has a leavening effect throughout the organization.

Among the many statements Laney made about the moral dimensions of an academic presidency, this is representative: "The moral authority of the president...consists of helping to keep alive the sense that the university exists by sufferance of society, and its graduates are to participate in the upbuilding of society and citizenship. The necessity of restraint, the quest for reality, and the obligation to serve [sic]."[62] Laney's moral practice and sagacity were demonstrated in several important ways: by the restraint he and his wife displayed in their personal living and his own example, which inspired staff and others, and his commitment to dialogue in the university on moral issues. In terms of his own personal restraint as president, Laney offered this observation:

> The president, I think, needs to invite a certain aura. I don't mean being self-righteous, but exercise restraint in terms of what they allow themselves to do. They have a lot of opportunities for indulgence, and I've never seen a president indulge himself when he didn't lose respect. It's

almost a direct correlation. Whether it's to build too grand a home or conspicuous consumption or if they even do too much in the office.[63]

In the president's home, for instance, Laney did not permit any renovation during his tenure, for he did not want it to appear that he was indulging himself at the expense of the rest of the university.

Laney's leadership demonstrated a model of fairness and integrity that won him the confidence and respect of his followers. In the discussion of charisma, it was noted how many of Laney's staff considered him as a mentor as well as a supervisor. Much of this was due to his personality and style. It was enhanced, as well, by his demonstration of making decisions in the best interests of the university. Hatcher shared with Ault that he had learned a great deal from Laney. Much of what he learned was that sacrifice, such as the financial tithe of the medical center to the university, is for the good of the whole, even though it is not second nature to make such a sacrifice. This led Ault to conclude that,

> This kind of influence—one by example more than exhortation, as it emanates through webs of contact and command in an organization—can have, I would suspect, considerable effect throughout an institution during one president's tenure. From my own dealings with many quarters and levels of the Emory life, I found a degree of honesty, cooperativeness, and generosity I have not been accustomed to see in academic life.[64]

Thus, by example, Laney's moral influence, enhanced by his Protestant and Southern upbringing, both attracted followers to him and inspired them to demonstrate attributes of fairness and integrity in their dealings with others.

Among Laney's greatest preoccupations was to develop the community of scholars he described in his inaugural address. The community of scholars was, for him, one committed to engaging the great moral issues of the day. In making this point, he wrote:

> College and university presidents have the opportunity to take initiative in establishing communities of moral discourse on their campuses. In this way, when those ostensibly alien issues like divestment or war or drugs or city crime surface on campus, not only will there be in place the means to communicate about them, but the issues themselves will appear less foreign to the life of the academy.[65]

In this respect, Laney was especially proud of the Freshman Seminar and the Luce Professors' Program, both of which fostered moral discourse on a variety of subjects. Laney also sought community discussions about apartheid in South Africa, rights of gays and lesbians, and racial issues on campus. Laney believed, too, that he as president would not grow nor give effective leadership if he did not offer himself for face-to-face time with groups that felt they were on the margins. As Laney reported to Ault, "...it's really hard for a white, middle-aged male to see that many changes in the way in which one— in what one considers in the process of decision [making] even with good intentions. You have to change your habits of decision making. [Thus,] I spend a lot of time in face-to-face where both of you really begin to see each other as people and not merely as types."[66]

While the manifestations of the moral community envisaged by Laney were present throughout his tenure, there is an irony that the community he sought was more akin to the old, regional Emory than the new, national Emory he was helping to create. As Fox-Genovese noted,

Laney wanted faculty to be mentors to students, while at the same time he wanted Emory "to be a national university in an age of specialization."[67] The press toward a more accomplished and nationally recognized faculty meant that a fracturing of community was inevitable. Ault notes in his video that the Emory history department's struggle with the presence of more faculty attending student prospectus presentations is characteristic of this tension. In response to the issue, one member of the department states, "I personally would like to see a sense of community....[but] the community, at the moment, doesn't exist, and we're doing fine without it."[68] Creating the moral community throughout the university was a nearly impossible task, given its complexity and the varying agendas, as noted by Cohen and March. Still, as Ault argues, that the history department was concerned at all with the moral dimensions of their engagements with students should be viewed positively.[69] Thus, Laney's commitment to the moral authority of the president did have impact throughout the organization.

At points in this chapter, comparisons have been made between the leadership of Laney and Hutchins. Hutchins' leadership at Chicago has been much chronicled and Dzuback's analysis, in particular, provides helpful points of comparison. Kerr says that "Hutchins was the last of the giants in the sense that he was the last of the university presidents who really tried to change his institution and higher education in any fundamental way."[70] Without taking anything away from Hutchins' leadership, it would seem that Kerr's analysis is premature. While not enough time has elapsed since Laney's administration to make the case that he, too, is an academic giant, it can be said that Laney helped to mold and shape Emory's growth in a way that propelled it into the elite twenty-five private universities in the United States. Furthermore, he insisted that accompanying this transition would be a commitment to moral leadership on his part and moral development on the part of students where service and the upbuilding of society are paramount. In years to come, it is possible that Laney's name will stand alongside the names of many of the great US academic presidents since the founding of Harvard.

Soon after the announcement of Laney's resignation from Emory, Frye had this observation to make about the totality of Laney's leadership that expresses in brief what this chapter has attempted to explore:

> In the quick and urgent pace of change, I think it is fair to say Dr. Laney did not always follow a process that relied upon building a broad consensus and participatory decision making. Had he done so, we would probably be years behind where we are now. On the other hand, he was very effective in conveying a sense of purpose, values, commitment, and confidence in the course of the University, and that's what kept us all going in the same direction. His charisma and rhetorical skills and his obvious clear vision of what a great university should be, led people to very willingly, for the most part, accept his leadership. There are always going to be some out there who think that process is more important than results. I might add that because of the great progress we've made, Emory is now ready for a more deliberate, participatory approach to decision making. We probably weren't 15 years ago; at least not without the risk that the opportunity given us during those years would slip out of our hands.[71]

While all of Laney's actions as leader did not necessarily satisfy his followers nor demonstrate the openness and consensus building one might expect of a leader, Laney is still remembered by those who worked with him principally as a moral leader. His speeches, articles, and actions as president of Emory give ample testimony to his commitment to moral leadership.

---

[1]Involuntary relationships such as that between master and slave fail to meet the test for leadership. In this case, the master cannot be considered a leader since the slave is not able to give her/his obedience freely.

[2]Max Weber, *The Theory of Social and Economic Organization*, trans. A. M. Henderson and Talcott Parsons (New York: Oxford University Press, 1947) 328.

[3]Weber, *The Theory of Social and Economic Organization*, 330–59.

[4]Given that trustees generally make the final determination about the person hired as president and the responsibility of continuing the president in office resides with them as well, it is appropriate to ask if trustees are followers or leaders. As we saw in chapter 1, presidential search committees in the latter twentieth century increasingly include the voice and vote of all the institution's constituents in the selection of a president, as a recommendation to the trustees of whom they should select. While selection of presidents is among the most important activities of the trustees, I contend that, in general and especially in doctoral universities, most trustees are followers. They select the person they believe best suited for the office, and entrust that individual with making decisions regarding the institution that they themselves—as a lay body—are not equipped to make. Thus, actions taken by trustees are often the result of the recommendation that the president makes to them. So, while trustees make final decisions on a number of matters, they generally look to follow the president's lead in the decisions they should make.

[5]James T. Laney, "The Moral Authority of the President," April 1983, *Heart*, 5–6.

[6]James A. Ault, Jr., *Leading Out Print Resources: A Video/Print Documentary on Leadership and Governance in Higher Education* (Northampton, MA: James Ault Productions, 1996), 29.

[7]Ault, *Leading Out Print Resources*, 30.

[8]All letters in Laney Papers, box 21, folder "Faculty," RWWL. See in order listed Don Saliers to James T. Laney, 5 October 1979; David Freides to James T. Laney, 8 October 1979; Nathaniel E. Gozansky to James T. Laney, 8 October 1979; Leon Mandell to James T. Laney, 5 October 1979.

[9]"Billy Frye Reflects on the Impact of the Laney Years," *Emory Report*, 46/7 (11 October 1993): 5.

[10]David Minter, telephone conversation with author, LaGrange GA, 7 July 1998.

[11]Billy E. Frye, interview by author, tape recording, Emory University, Atlanta, 23 June 1998;

[12]James T. Laney, interview by author, tape recording, Emory University, Atlanta, 11 November 1997.

[13]Laney interview, 11 November 1997.

[14]Michael D. Cohen and James G. March, "Leadership in an Organized Anarchy," *Organization and Governance in Higher Education: An ASHE Reader* (Needham Heights MA: Ginn Press, 1991) 400.

[15]Cohen and March, "Leadership in an Organized Anarchy," 406–11. Another tactical rule promoted by Charles Lindblom is for the president to learn the science of "muddling through" the administrative detail in bureaucracies so that critical goals and objectives are achieved. See Charles E. Lindblom, "The Science of 'Muddling Through,'" *Public Administration Review* 19/2 (Spring 1959): 79–88.

[16]Scott Plous, *The Psychology of Judgment and Decision Making* (Philadelphia: Temple University Press, 1993) 94–95.

[17]Laney interview, 11 November 1997.

[18]Frye and Minter interviews; John Temple, interview by author, note recording, Emory University, Atlanta, 17 July 1998; William H. Fox, interview by author, note recording, Emory University, Atlanta, 7 July 1998.

[19]Frye interview.

[20]J. Thomas Bertrand, July 1997, copyrighted personal notes, Brevard NC, in author's possession. Also Fox interview for a similar view.

[21]Temple interview.

[22]Laney interview, 17 August 1998.

[23]Laney interview, 17 August 1998.

[24]Ault, *Leading Out Print Resources*, 4.

[25]Frye, Fox, Temple, Minter interviews. Bertrand notes.

[26]Estella Bensimon and Anna Neumann, *Redesigning Collegiate Leadership: Teams and Teamwork in Higher Education* (Baltimore: Johns Hopkins University, Press, 1993) 19.

[27]Scott Plous, *The Psychology of Judgment and Decision Making* (Philadelphia: Temple University Press, 1993) 15.

[28]For an important discussion on the consequences of group-think see Plous, *The Psychology of Judgment and Decision Making*, 204–205.

[29]Ault, *Leading Out Print Resources*, 93. Ault writes, "Revising the Equal Opportunity Statement was…a tough and painful issue for some trustees and, I was told, cost Laney dearly in terms of 'the chips' he 'had to call in' to assure its passage."

[30]Frye interview.

[31]Frye interview.

[32]Jack S. Boozer to James T. Laney, 6 September 1979, Laney Papers, box 17, folder "AAUP," RWWL, 1.

[33]"Report to Emory Chapter, AAUP," 1 November 1979, Laney Papers, box 17, folder "AAUP," RWWL.

[34]Laney interview, 11 November 1997.

[35]Peter S. Baker to Billy E. Frye, 5 July 1990, Laney Papers, box 25-2, folder "College Dean Search Committee," RWWL.

[36]David Freides to Billy E. Frye, 19 June 1990, Laney Papers, box 25-2, folder "College Dean Search Committee," RWWL.

[37]Frye interview.

[38]Minter interview.

[39]Fox interview.

[40]In discussing the expectations he had of his staff, Laney said, "I am a big delegator. I don't think I am as bad as Ronald Reagan, but I would run him a close second. I really believe in giving good people lots of room" (Laney interview, 11 November 1997).

[41]Laurence Veysey, *The Emergence of the American University* (Chicago: University of Chicago Press, 1965) 367–68.

[42]Given the lack of diversity in the 1990s on such an important committee it is easy to be critical of Laney's lack of initiative in diversifying this body more; however, as Ault notes, a 1990 study of the Association of Governing Boards (AGB) shows that Emory's full board had a higher percentage of non-whites (10 percent) "than fourteen of eighteen of its peer institutions including Columbia, Cornell, Penn, Duke, Rochester, MIT, and Chicago, and only slightly fewer women than the median for the same group of institutions" (Ault, *Leading Out Print Resources*, 22). What Ault does not point out and what the AGB study does not address is the racial and gender make-up of executive committees, which, one has to observe, was not very balanced at Emory.

[43]Ault, *Leading Out Print Resources*, 76. It is interesting to note that the debate in 1997–1998 by the church and the Emory board over same-sex marriages in the university's chapels has its roots in this action. Had board deliberations been more public and open when the Equal Opportunity Statement was amended in 1993, the board in-fighting that occurred over same-sex marriages might have been avoided.

[44]Ault, *Leading Out Print Resources*, 42.

[45]Laney interview, 11 November 1997.

[46]James T. Laney to Development Office, 25 February 1991, Laney Papers, box 6-8, pt. 4, "Correspondence Notebook January–March 1991," RWWL, 2.

[47]Jay A. Conger, *The Charismatic Leader: Behind the Mystique of Exceptional Leadership* (San Francisco: Jossey Bass, Pubs., 1989).

[48]James L. Fisher and James V. Koch, *Presidential Leadership: Making a Difference* (Phoenix: Oryx Press, 1996) 25–26.

[49]Fox and Minter interviews as well as James Sibley, interview by author, note recording, Atlanta, 14 July 1998.

[50]Fox, Minter, Sibley, and Frye interviews. Bertrand notes.

[51]Minter interview.

[52]Fox interview.

[53]Ault, *Leading Out Print Resources*, 22.

[54]Bertrand notes.

[55]Frye interview. Laney confirmed this in an interview when he said, "I mean they had to please to me in the true sense, not in terms of my vanity, but they had to…be able to meet my expectations" (Laney interview, 11 November 1997).

[56]Laney interview, 11 November 1997.

[57]Ault, *Leading Out Print Resources*, 83.

[58]Marian Dearing, interview by author, note recording, Emory University, Atlanta, 8 October 1994.

[59]Fisher and Koch, *Presidential Leadership*, 34. They write, "…the leader moves around the organization frequently, being warm and friendly, but not overly involved or intimate, and always remaining on the platform. The president is always president."

[60]For a detailed analysis of Laney's view on the moral dimensions of a liberal arts education see chapter 2. Also see William J. Bennett, *The War Over Culture in Education* and *The De-Valuing of America: The Fight for Our Culture and Our Children*; Allan Bloom, *The Closing of the American Mind: How Higher Education Has Failed Democracy and Impoverished the Souls of Today's Students;* and Ernest Boyer, *Scholarship Reconsidered: The Priorities of the Professoriate.*

[61]Robert Michael Franklin, "Clergy Politics: The Black Experience," in James Wind, ed., *Clergy Ethics in a Changing Society* (Nashville: Abingdon Press, 1991) 281.

[62]Laney, "Moral Authority of the President," 11

[63]Laney interview, 11 November 1997.

[64]Ault, *Leading Out Print Resources*, 84.

[65]James T. Laney, "Presidential Leadership for Shared Values in Pluralist Communities: The Issue and the Challenge," January 1991, *Heart*, 29.

[66]Ault, *Leading Out Print Resources*, 74–75.

[67]Ault, *Leading Out Print Resources*, 74.

[68]Ault, *Leading Out Print Resources*, 73.

[69]Ault, *Leading Out Print Resources*, 89.

[70]Clark Kerr, *The Uses of the University*, third edition (Cambridge: Harvard University Press, 1982) 33.

[71]"Billy Frye Reflects on the Impact of the Laney Years," 5

CONCLUSION

The challenges of latter twentieth-century and early twenty-first-century higher education have presented many demands to academic presidents not faced by their counterparts, such as Eliot, Harper, Hutchins, and Bond, in earlier times. These challenges and the universities' responses have compelled contemporary scholars, such as Michael Katz, to worry that, unlike earlier generations, universities have abandoned their moral calling. About this concern, Katz writes:

> In the late nineteenth and early twentieth centuries, university expansion grafted bureaucracy onto corporate voluntarism; the form that emerged was the multiversity. Without a core of principles, the multiversity has been unable to resolve the great moral issues confronting it in recent decades. Instead, it drifts, pulled by tensions between democracy and bureaucracy, community and market-place. Increasingly bureaucracy and the market are winning....Therefore, the next great crisis of the university may not be demographic, fiscal, or organizational. Instead, it may be moral.[1]

Nelson agrees that university life has changed dramatically over the last century; yet, he does not concede that contemporary institutions have entirely lost their moral moorings. Through an exhaustive analysis of the speeches of nineteen academic presidents in the last century, including six presidents from the 1980s and 1990s, Nelson finds that the moral voice of the president, while different in the language used and often more tentative in the claims that are made, is at root concerned for the education of the hearts of students. While Nelson does not include Laney in his analysis of the six contemporary presidents, he does use some of Laney's articles extensively in assessing the contemporary scene. He credits Laney with giving contemporary attention to the expression "education of the heart," and he suggests that Laney is unique for his era in his continuous focus on the moral dimensions of academic leadership.[2]

For Laney, the moral relativism of the latter twentieth century has created a generation of academic presidents who, for the most part, do not see as among their greatest responsibilities to provide moral leadership for their institutions.[3] Yet, Laney's greatest passion while leading Emory was to create a sense among all of its constituent groups of the moral obligations inherent in all that the institution undertook. On how he viewed his role as a moral leader, Laney had this to offer:

> An educator is a moral leader; it is inescapable. That's just the name of the game, and not to see that, and therefore consciously fill that role, not in the sense of being good, but in the sense of being responsible to the students and to the institution seems to me to be an issue of great moment. What I'm talking about is the definition of the job, or the definition of the role of the president. It's just not a role that I arrogated to myself. It's a role that I said is inescapably a part of this job. I will accept it and use it. That's what I am trying to say. It's not that people are not extremely moral or high-minded. It's that they don't see that as a prominent part of their pantheon of responsibilities.... There is a profound reluctance to do

that. And yet, I think that [it is most important] to see that and to help the university to see itself as a moral institution, or an institution that is charged with perpetuating a moral sensibility.[4]

The analysis of Laney's speeches and articles in this book has shown the fervor with which he conveyed his views about the moral dimensions of education. And the analysis of the transformation he brought about at Emory as a leading private university, including the challenges he faced along the way, has shown the fundamentally moral nature of his actions while in office. We have noted, too, that because of personality and institutional considerations, Laney's actions did not always seem in keeping with how he described moral leadership. His failure to promote a curriculum· that would address the critics of higher education such as Bennett and Bloom, his handling of the Great Park and apartheid at Emory, his hierarchical leadership style as it related to team building, the absence of a significant presence of women and minorities among his senior staff and the trustees, and his charisma enhanced by a posture of distance and formality may not fit with present day sensibilities about how a moral leader should act. Yet, it seems a mischaracterization to take these examples and conclude that Laney did not exhibit moral leadership, for the record, in total, suggests otherwise. In sum, it seems that Laney was a perfect match for the Emory he inherited. His notions of what it would take to be a great university, by emphasizing the college and the graduate program, fueled by the largest philanthropic gift at that time, provided the ideal setting for the moral leadership Laney provided. These efforts were rewarded by the recognition of external authorities, such as *US News and World Report* and the elite Association of American Universities, albeit the latter recognition came one year after his departure.

Laney departed Emory in October 1993, responding to a request from US President William Clinton to serve as the US Ambassador to South Korea, a position he held until early 1997. His departure surprised some trustees because the $400 million capital campaign (many believing him to be the key to its success) was only one-half completed. Yet, many of these trustees and others who worked closely with Laney knew he was fatigued and ready for a change. The opportunity to return to the country which inspired his missionary heart seemed to be perfectly timed. An interim president, Billy E. Frye, was named for a year, and William Chace, president of Wesleyan University, was chosen as Laney's permanent successor.

Biographical Statement on Laney[5]

James Laney served as US Ambassador to Korea from 1993–1997 and before that was president of Emory University for sixteen years. As ambassador he was an active proponent of increased trade between the two countries with Korea becoming the US's fifth largest market. He was also active in security issues, coordinating former President Jimmy Carter's trip to Pyongyang in June of 1994 which resulted in a freeze of the nuclear program in North Korea. He was intimately involved in the four power initiative launched by Presidents Clinton and Kim at Cheju Island in April 1996, and the following month set forth its implications for US policy in major speeches at the Council on Foreign Relations in New York and the National Press Club in Washington. Upon completion of his tour in Korea, President Kim awarded him Korea's highest medal for diplomacy. He also received the Department of Defense highest civilian medal for distinguished public service and the James Van Fleet Award from the Korean Society.

During his tenure as president of Emory University, it emerged as a nationally recognized institution with one of the largest endowments among all universities. Before assuming the presidency of Emory, Dr. Laney served eight years as dean of the Candler School of Theology. An ordained United Methodist Minister, he served churches in Connecticut, Ohio, and Tennessee in the 1950s and 1960s.

Dr. Laney has spoken and published widely on issues of higher education and the place of ethics in the professions. His articles have appeared in the *Harvard Magazine, Vital Speeches* and the *New York Times,* as well as in books on higher education and scholarly journals. A collection of his addresses, *The Education of the Heart,* was published in 1994. He has spoken at major universities and seminaries around the country and abroad.

Dr. Laney has been awarded honorary degrees from nineteen institutions, including Yale, the University of St. Andrews in Scotland and Emory. He is also a graduate of Yale with honors degrees in economics and divinity, as well as a Ph.D. degree as a Macintosh Fellow. In 1996, he was awarded the Wilbur Cross medal by Yale for contributions to academic and public life.

He has been profiled in the *Wall Street Journal* and the *New York Times* and was featured in a documentary film on leadership in higher education.

He has chaired an Overseers Committee at Harvard and was a member of the Executive Committee of Yale University Council. He chairs the United Board of Christian Higher Education in Asia and is a trustee of the Harvard-Yencheng Foundation, the National Humanities Center, the Henry Luce Foundation, and CARE. He was a director of the Coca-Cola Company and the Trust Company of Georgia, as well as the Atlantic Council of the United States. He is a member of the Council on Foreign Relations.

He served in Korea in 1947–1948 in Army counterintelligence and again from 1959–1964 under the Methodist Church teaching at Yonsei University. Dr. Laney has maintained close ties to Korea through the years, returning often to lecture. He has also taught at Vanderbilt and Harvard.

Dr. Laney continues to be engaged in the Korean situation, serving as co-chair of the Council on Foreign Relations Task Force on Korea, making frequent trips to Asia in private and official capacities. He is a trustee of the Henry Luce Foundation, and chairs with Andrew Young the Faith and the City Program in Atlanta.

Ambassador Laney and his wife, the former Berta Radford, have five children and fifteen grandchildren. They reside in Atlanta.

---

[1]Michael B. Katz, *Reconstructing American Education* (Cambridge MA: Harvard University Press, 1987) 3, 180.

[2]Nelson, *A Study of the Moral Voice of the College President.* See pages 48–58 for his discussion of Laney's understanding of the moral voice of the academic president. Nelson's study looked at six higher education institutions and speeches given by three presidents of each institution dating back to the turn-of-the twentieth century, the mid 1900s and the 1980s and 1990s. The schools and the presidents (listed in chronological order) Nelson studies are: Amherst—George Harris, Peter Pouncy, Thomas Gerety; Clark Atlanta University—Horace Bumstead, William Crogman/Elias Blake, Jr., Thomas Cole, Jr.; Columbia University—Nicholas Murray Butler, Michael Sovern, George Rupp; Notre Dame University—James Cavanaugh, Theodore Hesburgh, Edward Malloy; University of Michigan—James Angell, Harold Shapiro, James Duderstadt; Wellesley College—Caroline Hazard, Nannerl Keohane, Diana Chapman Walsh.

[3]James T. Laney, interview by author, tape recording, Emory University, Atlanta, 17 August 1998.

[4]Laney interview, 17 August 1998.

[5]This biographical statement on Laney provides some details not covered by this book. This statement was provided by Laney's office in August 2000.

BIBLIOGRAPHY

Archival Materials
All archival materials are listed according to the collection in which they can be found, i.e. Bowden Papers, Laney Papers, White Papers, and Woodruff Papers. Unpublished articles and speeches by Laney are listed under "Laney, Unpublished Works," with complete bibliographic information. All archival materials used in this book are housed at the Special Collections Department, Robert W. Woodruff Library, Emory University, Atlanta. Emory University holds the copyright to all of these materials.

Henry Bowden Papers
Bowden, Henry to Gene Tucker and Albert Stone, 13 November 1975.
Brooks, D.W. to Henry Bowden, 22 October 1976.
Department Chairs to Charles Howard Candler, 3 April 1957.
Emory University Board of Trustee Minutes, 17 March 1977.
"Guidelines for the Selection of Emory University's President," May 1976.
Klein, Luella and Theodore Weber to Henry Bowden, 25 February 1977.
Tucker, Gene and Albert Stone to Henry Bowden, 11 November 1975.
Ward, Jake to Henry Bowden, 31 March 1976.
Ward, Jake to Henry Bowden, 18 January 1977.
Weber, Ted to Henry Bowden, 3 February 1977.

James T. Laney Papers
"Announcement by President James T. Laney At Monday or Tuesday Press Conference," no date. Box 23-2, "Correspondence Notebook April–June 1986."
Baker, Peter S. to Billy E. Frye, 5 July 1990. Box 25-2, folder "College Dean Search Committee."
Boozer, Jack S. to James T. Laney, 6 September 1979. Box 17, folder "AAUP."
"Emory, The Carter Center and the Issue of the Roadway Through the Great Park: A Chronology," no date. Box 23-3, "Correspondence Notebook April–June 1986."

"Emory University, Emily and Ernest Woodruff Endowment Fund Income Utilized for Enrichment Purposes 1981–82 through 1986–87," no date. Box 16-2, folder "Five Year Plan."

Freides, David to Billy E. Frye, 19 June 1990. Box 25-2, folder "College Dean Search Committee."

Freides, David to James T. Laney, 8 October 1979. Box 21, folder "Faculty."

Frye, Billy E. to Colleagues (academic deans), 6 April 1987. Box 5, folder "Graduate School."

Frye, Billy E. to James T. Laney, 4 February 1987. Box 5, folder "Graduate School."

"General Faculty Meeting," 1 February 1978. Box 21, folder "Faculty."

Gozansky, Nathaniel E. to James T. Laney, 8 October 1979. Box 21, folder "Faculty."

"Lamar Report: General Recommendations," 8 April 1982. Box 4/5, folder "Lamar Report."

Laney, James T. to Bishop Joel McDavid, 11 September 1985. Box 21-2, folder "South Africa."

Laney, James T. to Bishop Lloyd Knox, 26 September 1986. Box 21-2, folder "Campus Life."

Laney, James T. to Carl G. Renfroe, 8 June 1989. Box 27-1, folder "Commencement 1989."

Laney, James T. to Development Office, 25 February 1991. Box 6-8, pt. 4, "Correspondence Notebook January–March 1991."

Laney, James T. to Colleagues in Ministry, 16 November 1979. Box 16, folder "Pub."

Laney, James T. to the Emory Faculty, 16 January 1982. Box 23-2, "Correspondence Notebook April–June 1986."

Laney, James T. to George Rupp, 16 August 1985. Box 9, folder "Rice University Inauguration."

Laney, James T. to Jimmy Carter, 27 February 1985. Box 2, folder "AAU."

Laney, James T. to Robert E. Armstrong, 30 March 1992. Box 6-8, pt. 5, "Correspondence Notebook March–July 1992."

Laney, James T. to Robert Rosenzweig, 15 May 1987. Box 5, folder "Graduate School."

Laney, James T. to Robert Strickland, 3 May 1989. Box 6-8, pt. 1, "Correspondence Notebook May–June 1989."

Laney, James T. to Robert Strickland, 30 April 1990. Box 6-8, pt. 3, "Correspondence Notebook April–June 1990."

Laney, James T. to Roberto Goizeuta and Don Keough, 18 July 1986. Box 21-2, folder "South Africa."

Laney, James T. to the Emory students, faculty and staff, 19 November 1987. Box 4, folder "Equal Opportunity Program."

Laney, James T. to the faculties of Emory University, 13 March 1980. Box 22, folder "Woodruff Foundation."

Lester, Charles T. to Members of the Advisory Committee for the Evaluation of Emory's Capital Needs," 26 February 1979. Box 4, folder "Capital Needs Committee Report."

"A Letter From President Laney to the Emory Community," 17 April 1990. Box 38, folder "Collins, Sabrina."

Mallard, Bill and Gatra to James T. Laney, 25 April 1990. Box 38, folder "Collins, Sabrina."

Mandell, Leon to James T. Laney, 5 October 1979. Box 21, folder "Faculty."

Milton, Frances B. to James T. Laney, 23 April 1990. Box 38, folder "Collins, Sabrina."

"Minutes of the Investment Committee of the Board of Trustees of Emory University," 14 July 1987. Box 10, folder "BOT Misc."

"An Open Letter to the Atlanta Community Concerning Emory University: Draft," no date. Box 38, folder "Collins, Sabrina."

"Remarks by President James T. Laney to Students, Sunday Evening, April 22," 22 April no year. Box 38, folder "Collins, Sabrina."

Renfroe, Carl G. to James T. Laney, 18 May 1989. Box 27-1, folder "Commencement 1989."

"Report of the Advisory Committee for Evaluation of Emory's Capital Needs," 26 February 1979. Box 4.

"Report to Emory Chapter, AAUP," 1 November 1979. Box 17, folder "AAUP."

"Report to Faculty," 2 December 1982. Box 25-2, folder "Speaking Engagements 1985–85 [sic]."

"Resolution Proposed by Professor Dan Carter," no date. Box 23-2, "Correspondence Notebook April–June 1986."

Saliers, Don to James T. Laney, 5 October 1979. Box 21, folder "Faculty."

Shore, Brad to James T. Laney, 19 April 1990. Box 38, folder "Collins, Sabrina."

Silversmith, S.F. to James T. Laney, 25 July 1990. Box 38, folder "Collins, Sabrina."

"Statement of the African American Students of Emory University," no date. Box 38, folder "Collins, Sabrina."

Strickland, Robert to those concerned, 29 January 1985. Box 23-3, "Correspondence Notebook April–June 1986."

"Symposium Announcement," no date. Box 21, folder "Faculty."

"Transcription of Remarks Presented at the Trustee Retreat," 13–14 March 1987. Box 10, folder "Trustees Retreat 1987."

Theodore Weber Papers

Ward, Jake Memo to Emory Community, 17 May 1976. Personal Papers of Theodore Weber. Atlanta.

Goodrich C. White Papers
"Report to the Trustees Committee for the Selection of a President for the University," May 1956. Series I, box 18.

Robert W. Woodruff Papers
Jones, Boisfeuillet to Robert W. Woodruff, 11 April 1978. Robert W. Woodruff Alpha Files. Box 85, folder "Emory 1976–1985."
Laney, James T. to Robert W. Woodruff, 22 December 1977. Robert W. Woodruff Alpha Files. Box 85, folder 6.
Moore, Arthur J. to Robert W. Woodruff, 7 November 1957. Robert W. Woodruff Alpha Files. Box 85, folder 4.
"Prayer Offered at the Birthday Dinner of Mr. Robert W. Woodruff," 6 December 1978. Robert W. Woodruff Alpha Files. Document Case 10, Box "L," folder "Laney."
Woodruff, Robert W. to Bishop Arthur J. Moore, 5 November 1977. Robert W. Woodruff Alpha Files. Box 85, folder 4.
Woodruff, Robert W. to Henry L. Bowden, 5 October 1976. Robert W. Woodruff Alpha Files. Box 34, folder 13.
Woodruff, Robert W. to James T. Laney, not dated. Robert W. Woodruff Papers. Collection 10, Box 7, folder 2.

Interviews
Bowden, Henry. Interview by author, 2 March 1995. Tape recording. Emory University, Atlanta.
Dearing, Marian. Interview by author, 8 October 1994. Note recording. Emory University, Atlanta.
Fox, William H. Interview by author, 7 July 1998. Note recording. Emory University, Atlanta.
Frye, Billy E. Interview by author, 23 June 1998. Tape recording. Emory University, Atlanta.
Hatcher, Charles. Interview by author, 14 July 1998. Note recording. Emory University, Atlanta.
Lamar, Howard. Interview by author, 9 July 1998. Telephone conversation. LaGrange, Georgia.
Laney, James T. Interview by author, 11 November 1997, 23 June 1998, and 17 August 1998. Tape recordings. Emory University, Atlanta.
Minter, David. Interview by author, 7 July 1998. Telephone conversation. LaGrange, Georgia.
Sibley, James. Interview by author, 14 July 1998. Note recording. Atlanta.
Temple, John. Interview by author, 17 July 1998. Note recording. Atlanta.

Ward, Judson. Interview by author, 10 March 1995. Tape recording. Emory University, Atlanta.
Weber, Theodore. Interview by author, 1 March 1995. Note recording. Emory University, Atlanta.

Publications
"Alistair Cooke's Visit." *Emory Magazine* 54 (Winter Quarter 1978): 12.
Ault, James A., Jr. *Leading Out Print Resources: A Video/Print Documentary on Leadership and Governance in Higher Education.* Northampton MA: James Ault Productions, 1996.
Belenky, Mary Field. *Women's Ways of Knowing: The Development of Self, Voice, and Mind.* New York: Basic Books, 1986.
Bennett, William J. *The De-Valuing of America: The Fight for Our Culture and Our Children.* New York: Summitt Books, 1992.
———. *The War Over Culture in Education.* Washington, DC: Heritage Foundation, 1991.
Bensimon, Estella, and Anna Neumann. *Redesigning Collegiate Leadership: Teams and Teamwork in Higher Education.* Baltimore: Johns Hopkins University Press, 1993.
Bierle, Andrew W. M., "The Vision." *Emory Magazine* 69 (Winter 1994): 4–12.
"Billy Frye Reflects on the Impact of the Laney Years." *Emory Report* 46 (11 October 1993): 5.
Blau, Peter M., and Rebecca Zames Marguiles. "The Reputation of American Professional Schools." *Change Magazine* 6 (Winter 1974-1975): 42–47.
Bloom, Allan. *The Closing of the American Mind: How Higher Education Has Failed Democracy and Impoverished the Souls of Today's Students.* New York: Simon and Schuster, 1987.
Bowen, Howard R. and Jack H. Schuster. *American Professors: A National Resource Imperiled.* New York: Oxford University Press, 1986.
Boyer, Ernest L. *Scholarship Reconsidered: Priorities of the Professoriate.* Princeton: Carnegie Foundation for the Advancement of Teaching, 1990.
———. *The Undergraduate Experience in America.* New York: HarperCollins Pubs., 1987.
Briggs, Kenneth A. "Prized Theological Library Sold to Emory U. for $1.75 Million." *New York Times,* 21 August 1976, 23.
Bullock, Henry M. *A History of Emory University.* Nashville: Parthenon Press, 1936.
Cannon, William R. *A Magnificent Obsession: The Autobiography of William Ragsdale Cannon.* Nashville: Abingdon Press, 1999.
"Celebrity Professors: Do They Pay Off for Colleges and Students?" *Newsweek on Campus* (September 1987): 9.
Coe, Elizabeth. "Laney Announces Fund Drive." *The Wheel,* October 1979, 9.

Cohen, Michael D., and James G. March. "Leadership in an Organized Anarchy." *Organization and Governance in Higher Education: An ASHE Reader*. Needham Heights MA: Ginn Press, 1991.

Conger, Jay A. *The Charismatic Leader: Behind the Mystique of Exceptional Leadership*. San Francisco: Jossey Bass, Publishers, 1989.

Cummings, Judith. "New President is Elected at Cornell." *New York Times*, 17 February 1977, 34.

Denzin, Norman K. *Interpretative Biography*. Newbury Park CA: SAGE Publications, Inc., 1989.

Dzuback, Mary Ann. *Robert M. Hutchins: Portrait of an Educator*. Chicago: University of Chicago Press, 1991.

"Emory Benefactor Accepts 37 Year Old Honorary." *Emory Magazine* (Fall Quarter 1979): 7.

Fisher, James L., and James V. Koch. *Presidential Leadership: Making a Difference*. Phoenix: Oryx Press, 1996.

Frank, Thomas Edward. "Conserving a Rational World: Theology, Ethics, and the Nineteenth Century American Ideal." Ph.D. dissertation, Emory University, 1981.

Franklin, Robert Michael. "Clergy Politics: The Black Experience." James Wind, ed. *Clergy Ethics in a Changing Society*. Nashville: Abingdon Press, 1991.

Frye, Billy E., "Introduction: Emory and the Crisis in American Higher Education." *Emory Report* 47 (26 September 1994): 2.

————. *A Vision for Emory: A Report from the Chancellor*. Atlanta: Emory University, 1998.

Geertz, Clifford. "Deep Play: Notes on the Balinese Cockfight." *Daedaleus: Journal of the American Academy of Arts and Sciences* 101 (Winter 1972): 1–37.

Gilligan, Carol. *In a Different Voice: Psychological Theory and Women's Development*. Cambridge MA: Harvard University Press, 1982.

Graham, Hugh, and Nancy Diamond. *The Rise of American Research Universities: Elites and Challengers in the Postwar Era*. Baltimore: Johns Hopkins University Press, 1997.

Hardie, Ann. "Volunteer, Nunn Urges Graduates." *Atlanta Journal and Constitution*, 16 May 1989, B3.

Hauk, Gary, and Sandra J. Still, eds. *The Education of the Heart: Selected Speeches of James T. Laney*. Atlanta: Emory University, 1994.

————. *A Legacy of Heart and Mind: Emory Since 1836*. Atlanta: Emory University, 1999.

Hawkins, Hugh. *Between Harvard and America: The Educational Leadership of Charles W. Eliot*. New York: Oxford University Press, 1991.

hooks, bell. *Talking Back: Thinking Feminist, Thinking Black*. Boston: South End Press, 1989.

Hutchins, Robert Maynard. *Freedom, Education and the Fund: Essays and Addresses, 1946–1956.* New York: Meridan Books, 1956.

————. *The Higher Learning in America.* New Yaven: Yale University, 1936; reprint, New Brunswick NJ: Transaction Publishers, 1995.

Katz, Michael B. *Reconstructing American Education.* Cambridge MA: Harvard University Press, 1987.

Kemeny, Jean. *It's Different at Dartmouth.* Brattleboro VT: The Stephen Greene Press, 1979.

Kerr, Clark. *The Uses of the University: Third Edition.* Cambridge MA: Harvard University Press, 1982.

Kridel, Craig, ed. *Writing Educational Biography: Explorations in Qualitative Research.* New York: Garland Publishing, Inc., 1998.

Leape, Jonathan, Bo Baskin, and Stefan Underhill. *Business In the Shadow of Apartheid: US Firms in South Africa.* Lexington MA: Heath and Company, 1985.

Levine, David R. *The American College and the Culture of Aspiration, 1915–1940.* Ithaca NY: Cornell University Press, 1986.

Lindblom, Charles E. "The Science of Muddling Through." *Public Administration Review* 19/2 (Spring 1959): 79–88.

McArthur, Benjamin. "A Gamble on Youth: Robert M. Hutchins, the University of Chicago and the Politics of Presidential Selection." *History of Education Quarterly* 30 (Summer 1990): 161–86.

McLaughlin, Judith Black. "From Secrecy to Sunshine: An Overview of Presidential Search Practice." *Research in Higher Education* 22 (1985): 195–208.

McMillen, Liz. "Transformation of Emory: A Small Atlanta Institution is Using a Historic Gift to Vault into Big-Time Ranks." *Chronicle of Higher Education* 26 (27 September 1989): A1, A36–A38.

"National Universities: The Best Big Schools." *US News and World Report,* 26 October 1987, 53; 10 October 1988, C6; 28 September 1992, 114–15; 4 October 1993, 110–11.

Nelson, Stephen James. "A Study of the Moral Voice of the College President." Ph.D. dissertation, University of Connecticut, 1996.

Oates, Stephen, ed. *Biography as High Adventure: Life-Writers Speak on Their Art.* Amherst: University of Massachusetts Press, 1986.

Plous, Scott. *The Psychology of Judgment and Decision Making.* Philadelphia: Temple University Press, 1993.

"Preface to the Issue: Intellect and Imagination." *Daedalus. Journal of the American Academy of Arts and Sciences.* 109 (Spring 1980): v–viii.

"A Pub at Emory." *Atlanta Journal and Constitution Magazine,* 1 April 1979, 6.

"Racial Attack Leaves Freshman in Severe Shock." *New York Times,* 22 April 1990, I-44.

Ross, Marlene, and Madeleine F. Green. *The American College President: 1998 Edition.* Washington, DC: American Council on Education, 1998.

Rudolph, Frederick. *The American College and University: A History.* New York: Alfred A. Knopf, Inc., 1983.

Storr, Richard. *Harper's University: The Beginning.* Chicago: University of Chicago Press, 1966.

Traylor, Nick. "Emory University on the Rise." *Atlanta Magazine* (May 1982) 73–76, 108–110.

Urban, Wayne. *Black Scholar: Horace Mann Bond 1904–1972.* Athens: University of Georgia Press, 1992.

Veysey, Laurence. *The Emergence of the American University.* Chicago: University of Chicago Press, 1965.

Weber, Max. *The Theory of Social and Economic Organization.* Trans. by A. M. Henderson and Talcott Parsons. New York: Oxford University Press, 1947.

Wycliff, Don. "Emory Raises Its Status." *New York Times,* 23 August 1990, A18.

Unpublished Work

Bertrand, J. Thomas. July 1997. Copyrighted personal notes of Bertrand. Brevard, North Carolina. In author's possession.

Frost, Susan H. "Emory University 1977, 1984, 1992 (Academic Year): Selected Indicators of Change," February 1994. Office of Institutional Planning and Research, Emory University, Atlanta. See following reports and charts in order in which they appear in document:

Emory University Regular, Full-Time Faculty Headcount, 1977–1992 (Academic Years).

Emory College Geographic Distribution of Freshmen, 1977–1992.

Changing Circumstances and Views of Freshmen: Emory and Highly Selective Private Universities.

Emory College, Characteristics of Entering Students, 1987–1992.

Selected Findings of the Cooperative Institutional Research Program Freshman Survey (CIRP).

Emory University Enrollment, 1977–1992 (Academic Years).

Emory and Other Private Universities, Fall, 1977–Fall, 1992.

Emory College Enrollment History, Fall, 1977–Fall, 1993.

Emory University Graduate School of Arts and Sciences, Ph.D. Degrees Awarded, 1977–1993.

The Woodruff Health Sciences Center Sponsored Research, Fiscal, 1998–Fiscal, 1993.

Sponsored Research Topped $100M Last Year. Sponsored Research Total and Federal Obligations, Fiscal, 1987–Fiscal, 1993.

Campus Life Reflects a Vigorous University.

Emory University Financial Highlights, 1977–78 to 1992–93.

Emory University Financial Highlights, 1977–1993.

Emory and Selected Private Universities Spending on Educational Program Per Student.

Emory University Total Tuition and Student Aid, 1977–1993.

Emory Focuses on Excellence as the ACE Recommends that Universities Restructure.

James T. Laney's Published Works

Laney, James T. "Birthright and Blessing," May 1992. *The Education of the Heart: Selected Speeches of James T. Laney.* Atlanta: Emory University, 1994. (Hereafter, all articles in this publication will be designated by *Heart.*)

———. "Choose Your Dreams Wisely," May 1981. *Emory Magazine* (Fall 1981).

———. "The Distinction Between a Lifestyle and a Life," May 1987. *Heart.*

———. "Education and the Common Good," 30 March 1989. Laney Papers. Box 25-1, pocket 4. RWWL.

———. "The Education of the Heart," October 1984. *Heart.*

———. *Free Speech and the Freedom to Speak.* Presidential Papers, vol. 6, no. 1. Nashville: Division of Higher Education and Ministry, Board of Higher Education and Ministry, United Methodist Church, April 1990.

———. "A Future for Research." *Emory Magazine* (Fall Quarter 1977).

———. "Hope and Purpose for this Day." *Emory Magazine* (Fall Quarter 1992).

———. "How is Jesus the Lord of History?" Joe Hale, ed. *Proceedings of the Sixteenth World Methodist Conference.* Lake Junaluska: World Methodist Council, 1992.

———. "The Law: A Moral Aristocracy," March 1993. *Heart.*

———. "Liberal Arts Colleges and the Future of Higher Education," April 1989. *Heart.*

———. "Mending the Social Fabric: A Baccalaureate Address." *Emory Magazine* (Summer Quarter 1992).

———. *Mitre and Mortar Board: What Happens When the Ancient Office of Bishop Meets the Modern American College Board of Trustees.* Occasional Papers, no. 78. Nashville: United Methodist Board of Higher Education and Ministry, June 1989.

———. "Moral Authority in the Professions," March 1986. *Heart.*

———. "The Moral Authority of the President," April 1983. *Heart.*

———. *The Moral Purpose of the University.* Indianapolis: The Lilly Endowment, 1995.

———. "A New Way of Seeing for a New Global Society," May 1990. *Heart.*

———. "The Other Adam Smith." *Economic Review* (October 1981).

———. "The Possibilities of Limits," May 1993. *Heart.*

————. "Power and Moral Authority: A Baccalaureate Address." *Emory Magazine* (Summer Quarter 1993).

————. "Presidential Leadership for Shared Values in Pluralist Communities: The Issue and the Challenge," January 1991. *Heart.*

————. "The Purpose of a University Divinity School," April 1983. *Heart.*

————. *Our Mission in Higher Education: Vision and Reality.* Presidential Papers, vol. 8 no. 3. Nashville: Division of Higher Education, Board of Higher Education and Ministry, United Methodist Church, September 1992.

————. "Evaluating Liberal Education," July 1988. *Heart.*

————. "A Sense of Larger Purpose: A Sesquicentennial Convocation Address." *Emory Magazine* (March 1987).

————. "Success in the Service of an Important Cause," August 1988, *Heart.*

————. "Through Thick and Thin: Two Ways of Talking About the Academy and Moral Responsibility." In *Ethics in Higher Education,* ed. William W. May, 49–66. New York: American Council on Education, 1990.

————. "The Tree That Gives Good Fruit," *Emory Magazine* (August 1989).

————. "The True Nature of Authority: A Baccalaureate Address," *Emory Magazine* (July 1985).

————. "Why Tolerate Campus Bigots?" *New York Times,* 6 April 1990, A35.

James T. Laney's Unpublished Works

Laney, James T. "Address Given to the General Board of Global Ministries," 12 March 1984. Laney Papers. Box 25-1, pocket 2. RWWL.

————. "Address to Northside Kiwanis Club," 23 September 1977. Laney Papers. Box 25-1, pocket 1. RWWL.

————. "Address to Parents of Freshman Class '92," 27 August 1988. Laney Papers. Box 25-1, pocket 4. RWWL.

————. "Address to Rotary Club of Atlanta," 3 October 1977. Laney Papers. Box 25-1, pocket 1. RWWL.

————. "Annual Meeting of Board of Visitors: James T. Laney Remarks," 23 April 1986. Laney Papers. Box 25-1, pocket 3. RWWL.

————. "Annual Meeting of Board of Visitors: James T. Laney Remarks," 12 May 1993. Laney Papers. Box 25-1, pocket 7. RWWL.

————. "Baccalaureate Address, Emory University," 10 June 1977. Laney Papers. Box 25-1, pocket 1. RWWL.

————. "Baccalaureate Address, Emory University," June 1979. Laney Papers. Box 2, pocket 1. RWWL.

————. "Baccalaureate Sermon, Emory University," May 1984. Laney Papers. Box 34C, folder 1.10. RWWL.

————. "Board of Visitors," 13 May 1992. Laney Papers. Box 25-1, pocket 7. RWWL.

———. "Chairman's Message to the Annual Meeting of the United Board for Christian Higher Education in Asia," June 1990. Laney Papers. Box 21-2, folder UBCHEA. RWWL.

———. "Conference on Moral Values in Higher Education," 12–14 February 1987. Laney Papers. Box 25-1, pocket 3. RWWL.

———. "Dr. Laney's Notes from His Speech at the Southeastern Council on Foundations," 29 October 1981. Laney Papers. Box 25-2, folder "Speaking Engagements 1985–1986."

———. "Education as Identification," 9 November 1977. Laney Papers. Box 25-1, pocket 1. RWWL.

———. "Graduation Address: Westminster Schools," 16 May 1992. Laney Papers. Box 25-1, pocket 7, RWWL.

———. "Laney Contribution to the Randolph-Macon Sequicenntial [sic] Celebration Volume," January 1980. Laney Papers. Box 25-1, pocket 1. RWWL.

———. "Message from the Chair to the United Board of Christian Higher Education in Asia," July 1992. Laney Papers. Box 21-2, folder UBCHEA. RWWL.

———. "Oxford College Graduation," 11 June 1977. Laney Papers. Box 25-1, pocket 1, RWWL.

———. "President Laney's Speech to the Emory University Board of Visitors," 16 May 1990. Laney Papers. Box 25-1, pocket 6.

———. "'The Purpose of the College': Reaffirming the Wofford/Emory Ideal for the 21st Century,"19 February 1991. Laney Papers. Box 2, pocket 6. RWWL.

———. "Religion and the Open University: A Report From the Front," no date. Laney Papers. Box 25-1, pocket 6. RWWL.

———. "Remarks in Response to Installation," March 1978. Laney Papers. Box 25-2, folder "Correspondence, Speeches, and Clippings." RWWL.

———. "Remarks to General Faculty Assembly," September 1989. Laney Papers. Box 25-1, pocket 5. RWWL.

———. "Speech to the Southeastern Jurisdictional Assembly of the United Methodist Church," 15 July 1988. Laney Papers. Box 25-1, pocket 4. RWWL.

———. "An Unlikely Strength: A Baccalaureate Sermon," May 1983. Laney Papers. Box 34C, folder 1.9. RWWL.

INDEX